WEAPON

THE M14 BATTLE RIFLE

LEROY THOMPSON

Series Editor Martin Pegler

First published in Great Britain in 2014 by Osprey Publishing,
PO Box 883, Oxford, OX1 9PL, UK
PO Box 3985, New York, NY 10185-3985, USA
E-mail: info@ospreypublishing.com

OSPREY PUBLISHING IS PART OF THE OSPREY GROUP

A CIP catalog record for this book is available from the British
Library

Print ISBN: 978 1 4728 0255 2
PDF ebook ISBN: 978 1 4728 0256 9
ePub ebook ISBN: 978 1 4728 0257 6

Index by Mark Swift
Typeset in Sabon and Univers
Battlescenes by Johnny Shumate
Cutaway artwork by Alan Gilliland
Originated by PDQ Media, Bungay, UK
Printed in China through Worldprint Ltd

14 15 16 17 18   10 9 8 7 6 5 4 3 2 1

Osprey Publishing is supporting the Woodland Trust, the UK's
leading woodland conservation charity, by funding the dedication
of trees.

www.ospreypublishing.com

Acknowledgments
The author would like to thank the following for their assistance:
Ken Choate, Gina McNeely, John Miller, T.J. Mullin, National
Archives and Records Administration, Blake Stevens, Collector
Grade Publications, NRA Museums, Deb Williams.

Editor's note
In this book a mixture of metric and US customary measurements
is used. For ease of comparison please use the following
conversion table:

1 mile = 1.6km
1yd = 0.91m
1ft = 0.30m
1in = 2.54cm/25.4mm
1lb = 0.45kg

Cover images: (top) an M14 rifle (NRA Museums,
NRAmuseums.com); (bottom) September 2009, Afghanistan:
A member of the 82nd Airborne Division fires a fixed-sight M14,
which he has camouflaged to match the local terrain (US DOD).
Title page image: A demonstration of firing the T44 rifle during
April 1958. (NARA)

CONTENTS

INTRODUCTION

The M14 rifle shares with the M1892–99 Krag rifle the distinction of having been a standard US service rifle for only a decade or so. However, unlike the Krag, the M14 has proven a phoenix that has risen again during the "War on Terror" as a designated marksman rifle (DMR). Designed for a ground war in Western Europe, the M14 proved heavy and unwieldy in a jungle conflict in Vietnam. Therefore, it was replaced by the 5.56×45mm M16 rifle. During the conflict in Southeast Asia, the light weight and shorter overall length of the M16, combined with its smaller and lighter cartridge that allowed the infantryman to carry a greater basic ammunition load, made it a desirable replacement for the heavier M14. However, in Vietnam there were criticisms of the 5.56×45mm round's killing power.

While the M16 replaced the M14 in Southeast Asia, the M14 remained the standard-issue rifle in Europe for a few years, as its 7.62×51mm round was NATO (North Atlantic Treaty Organization) standard. By 1970, however, the M16 was replacing the M14 with troops assigned to Europe as well. Most M14s went into storage, though some were converted to M21 sniping rifle configuration. The US Special Forces would also develop their own sniper version of the M14 designated the M25. For a time in Vietnam, some US Marine Corps (hereafter USMC) units retained the M14 for use as a squad automatic weapon (SAW), much as they had previously used the Browning Automatic Rifle (BAR).

The M14 saw at least some usage with special-operations forces as it offered more knockdown power and range than the M16. Interestingly, the M14 became an "enemy" weapon, too, as "Opposing Force" OPFOR units at the Joint Readiness Training Center in Louisiana used the M14 as their rifle to differentiate them from US troops using the M16 or M4. The 3rd US Infantry Regiment's 1st Battalion has been issued the M14 for many years, as it uses M14s for ceremonial duties around Washington, DC. US Navy Honor Guards at the Pearl Harbor Memorials also use the M14. Combat in Afghanistan, however, was the greatest impetus to

During Operation *Junction City*, which ran from February to May 1967 in South Vietnam, a US soldier armed with an M14 watches a supply drop. (NARA)

issuing the M14 in substantial numbers decades after it had been relegated to storage in armories. The greater distances at which troops were engaging in Afghanistan made a rifle capable of longer ranges and greater striking power at those ranges vital, and engendered a renaissance for the M14. In fact, thousands have been issued for use as DMRs to US troops in Afghanistan and elsewhere. Other users in Afghanistan and Iraq have been US EOD (explosive ordnance device) personnel, who have used the 'scoped M14 SMUD (stand-off munition disrupter) to destroy IEDs (improvised explosive devices) or other explosives from a distance.

The US Navy has continued to use M14 rifles for shipboard security, but also for shooting mines at some distance from the ship. The Navy has also found that M14s, in some cases of DMR type with 'scopes, are effective to support VBSS (visit, board, search, and seizure) operations as well as other anti-piracy missions. As well as the Navy, the US Coast Guard uses its own version of the M14 with a 22in barrel and special muzzle brake.

Armed with the M14 rifle, trainees at Fort McClellan, Alabama, receive bayonet training during basic training in May 1966. (NARA)

What makes the M14 especially intriguing is that it is one of the shortest-lived US military weapons in terms of being the standard service rifle, yet arguably it ranks as the longest-serving US military rifle. Various US rifles had short service lives, including several Springfield percussion arms that each served for less than ten years. Early breech-loading Springfield rifles also had short service lives, in the case of the Model 1868 only four years. Even the Springfield M1892–99 Krag rifle only served as a standard weapon for about a decade. In the 20th century, however, with the exception of the M14, rifles served much longer. Despite the fact that the M1903 Springfield was superseded by the M1 Garand as the US Army's primary weapon in 1936, it continued in service into the 1950s or a bit later as a sniping rifle and on some US Navy ships. Although the M1 Garand served from 1936 until being replaced by the M16 in the 1960s, Garands also remained in limited service aboard US Navy ships and in some National Guard armories. Reportedly, some M1D sniping rifles were still around in the late 1980s. Of course, the M16 has been in service since 1962.

The M14 entered service in 1959 and by 1967 had been designated as a "Limited Standard" weapon, though it was still used by US troops in Europe until at least 1970. However, its use as a sniping rifle and DMR, as well as for other specialized tasks, has actually given it a service life of 54 years at the time of writing. As a result, the M14 ranks with the M1903

Springfield as the rifle that has remained in US service the longest, though the M16/M4 is on track to pass the M1903 soon.

During World War II, the semiautomatic M1 Garand had proven a formidable weapon, which gave US infantrymen a marked advantage over enemies armed with bolt-action rifles. Admittedly, German weapons such as the StG 44 heralded the future of infantry assault rifles, but they were not fielded early enough or in enough numbers to stave off German defeat. While World War II was still in progress, US ordnance personnel had solicited experimental models of the Garand, which would take a detachable magazine and incorporate full-automatic capability. In the immediate post-war years, various prototype rifles were developed incorporating these two features.

An important aspect of this development was the 7.62×51mm NATO round, which was based on the .300 Savage cartridge while retaining the case head of the World War II .30-06 cartridge and the same bullet diameter. A prototype rifle designated the T44 was chambered for this cartridge and incorporated select-fire capability and a 20-round detachable box magazine. Testing during 1952–53 narrowed the field to two designs: the US T44 and the Belgian T48 (the FN FAL). Although both rifles proved acceptable, the T44 was adopted because it was lighter, had fewer parts, and had a self-regulating gas system. It was also a US design. Adopted in 1957 as the M14, it went into production in 1959, with 1,376,031 M14 rifles eventually being produced. Because of US insistence on the 7.62×51mm round as NATO standard, development of the M14 would also influence two of the most important post-World War II rifle designs – the FN FAL and the German G3. Like the FAL and the G3, the M14 is a "battle rifle," one that is chambered for a full-power cartridge.

Contributing to the M14's staying power has been the high-quality semiautomatic versions of the rifle produced as the M1A by Springfield Armory – which, it should be noted, is not the US armory of that name, but a private company. Although the M14 is a select-fire weapon, during its service life it was issued to most soldiers with the selector switch removed so it could only be fired in semiautomatic mode. As a result, the semiautomatic M1A is very close to the M14 that was issued. Springfield Armory also produces a version of the M21 sniping rifle and other variants of the M1A.

As the last US general-issue battle rifle, the M14 holds an important place in US arms history. Many, too, consider it the best infantry rifle ever issued to US troops. Certainly, its long and active life over the last four decades is indicative that it continues to offer the shooter many advantages on the modern battlefield.

An Honor Guard from the US 3rd Infantry Regiment on duty at the Tomb of the Unknowns armed with M14 rifles with fixed bayonets. (US Army)

DEVELOPMENT
Replacing the Garand

During World War II, despite the great respect felt by most US infantrymen for the M1 Garand, there were some perceived shortcomings. Most notably, these included the lack of a higher-capacity detachable box magazine and the lack of select-fire capability. Some unit armorers did experiment with altering the M1 Garand to take BAR magazines and operate in full-automatic mode. In some cases, these conversions were fitted with bipods designed for the British Bren light machine gun. US Ordnance personnel had also experimented with giving the Garand more firepower. As early as 1942, John Garand himself had altered his rifle to take a BAR magazine, to use a modified BAR barrel, and to be capable of selective fire (Johnston & Nelson 2010: 959). The popularity of the M1 carbine, despite its relatively anemic .30 Carbine chambering, also offered an impetus to develop a lighter primary infantry rifle.

Another influence on US rifle development was examination by Ordnance Intelligence personnel of the German FG 42 and StG 44 rifles. As a result of examination of the FG 42 select-fire battle rifle, developed for German airborne troops, Springfield Armory and Remington Arms both began development of an airborne rifle based on the M1 Garand but having select-fire capability, a 20-round magazine capacity, a weight of 9lb or less without magazine, a folding stock, and in .30-06 caliber (Johnston & Nelson 2010: 560). Springfield Armory had already tested a rifle incorporating the shorter barrel and folding stock as the M1E5 (Stevens 1995: 26). These requirements evolved by September 1944, to require 15,000 lighter, more compact M1 Garands designed for airborne troops. Based on a prototype from Springfield Armory, a rifle designated the T26 was developed to meet this requirement. However, before it entered production World War II ended.

A presentation of the first M14 rifle by General Lyman L. Lemnitzer, Army Chief of Staff (left), to General David M. Shoup, Commandant of the USMC (right), on March 4, 1960. Holding the rifle is Sergeant Major Francis D. Rauber of the USMC. During the presentation of the rifle, it was optimistically billed as the replacement for the M1 rifle, M1 carbine, BAR, and M3A1 SMG (submachine gun). (NARA)

PRECURSORS TO THE M14

The T20, T22, and T23

Nevertheless, development of a new rifle based on the Garand continued. In 1944 Springfield Armory had developed a rifle designated the T20 for testing (Iannamico 2005: 24; Stevens 1995: 28). Firing from a closed bolt in semiautomatic mode and an open bolt in full-automatic mode, it used a modified BAR magazine and incorporated a muzzle brake that locked the gas cylinder in position. A primary consideration for Garand was to retain the BAR magazine, thus allowing interchangeability. Remington's T22 prototype was also sent to the US Army's Aberdeen Proving Ground in Maryland for testing, which indicated that the magazine and magazine catch needed to be strengthened on both rifles (Iannamico 2005: 24). John Garand determined that rather than redesigning the magazine, the receiver should be lengthened by .3125in, thus allowing the cartridges to feed much more reliably (Iannamico 2005: 24). Improvements were made to the magazine, and a new muzzle brake, which allowed attachment of a bayonet, was developed on the T20E1. Successful testing in 1945 resulted in an order for 100 of the improved version of the rifle for further testing. Though this order eliminated the folding stock and shorter barrel, the weapon retained select-fire capability and the 20-round magazine (Stevens 1995: 29). Further improvements were incorporated into the T20E2. T20E2 magazines would fit the BAR, but BAR magazines would not fit the T20E2. A bolt hold-open device was also incorporated. To aid in control, it had a cyclic rate reducer (to 700rds/min) for full-automatic fire (Johnston & Nelson 2010: 962). The T20E2 was well over the 9lb requirement, at 12.5lb. However, on May 17, 1945, the Ordnance Technical Committee recommended that 100,000 T20E2 rifles be acquired and designated Rifle, Caliber .30 M2. The war ended before they could be delivered (Iannamico 2005: 28).

9

A comparison between the semiautomatic M1A version of the M14 (top) and the M1 Garand at bottom shows the difference in size between the two rifles. (Author)

Development had also continued on Remington's T22; the T22E2 did not use the longer receiver and, hence, could use standard M1 Garand receivers and many of the same parts, an advantage since it would not require production of a different receiver. However, the T22E2 project was terminated in March 1948 (Iannamico 2005: 28). The T23 rifle was developed as a modification of the M1 Garand, but was ended in March 1945. Remington development continued with the T24, essentially a light machine gun which fired from a closed bolt in both modes of fire, but continued to use the eight-round Garand clip. The T24, too, was discarded, owing to the length of the .30-06 cartridge.

The T25 and T27

For more than a decade after the end of World War II, the USA continued to use the M1 Garand as its primary infantry weapon. However, development of a replacement continued. An important element of the rifle that would replace the M1 Garand was an improved cartridge to replace the .30-06 round. This was the T65 round, which was based on the .300 Savage cartridge and fired a 147-grain (9.5g) bullet at 2,750ft/sec (840m/sec), but with an overall length .5in (13mm) shorter than the .30-06 round.

Designed to fire the T65 cartridge, the T25 rifle, developed from September 1945 (Iannamico 2005: 31), was designed to be lightweight – only 7.5lb – and fire on either semi- or full-automatic, the latter from an open bolt. During testing the T25 performed well, but it proved too light to be controlled in full-automatic mode (Iannamico 2005: 31). At least partially due to the continuing Ordnance Department bias towards the M1 Garand, the T25 project was terminated in November 1951. However, soon after the ending of the T25 project – and five years before the adoption of the M14 – the Operations Research Office at Johns Hopkins University, Maryland, which had been established by the Pentagon to help evaluate new weapons concepts, issued the Hitchman report, which questioned the entire concept on which the M14 was based. This June 1952 report by Norman A. Hitchman, named "ORO-T-160: Operational Requirements for an Infantry Hand Weapon," drew conclusions based on the Army's files relating to World War II casualties and interviews with combat veterans of World War II and Korea, as well as other sources. As summarized by Hallahan in *Misfire*, these conclusions were:

– The rifle was most frequently effective at less than three hundred yards

– Most infantry kills were done by rifle at ranges under one hundred yards

– Marksmanship with a rifle is satisfactory only up to one hundred yards. Beyond that, it tails off to a low of three hundred yards.

– Hits could be significantly increased by replacing slow, aimed fire with weapons using the pattern dispersion principle at ranges up to three hundred yards, i.e. an automatic weapon spraying shots. More firepower; less aiming.

– The very expensive, finished weapon the American armory was turning out was over engineered and could be made cheaper without significant loss in hit effectiveness.

– Smaller calibers can do as much wounding as the .30 can – and do it with significant logistical and military gains over the .30 caliber.

– The smaller caliber with low recoil could improve dispersion control and hit probability over the higher recoil of the .30 caliber.

– Rifles like the T20 and T25 were valueless on separated man-sized targets.

– The Army in Korea, armed with the M1 semiautomatic rifle, was being outgunned by North Koreans with automatic weapons.

– All future wars would be characterized by close combat; long-range firing would be useless.

– Therefore, the American infantryman needed to be armed with maximum firepower for close-range fighting, i.e. a low-caliber, high-volume automatic rifle. (Hallahan 1994: 432)

Though many of the conclusions in this report may be questioned, especially in light of combat in Afghanistan, it is noteworthy for highlighting the constant battle that would have to be fought throughout the development of the M14 against the cadre of small-caliber advocates.

In April 1946, the T27 project was started by Remington Arms. This rifle was chambered for the T65 cartridge, but retained the M1's eight-round capacity. As with many of the other experimental designs, this one did not progress past prototypes and was terminated in March 1948 (Iannamico 2005: 32).

The T28, T31, T33, T34, T35, T36, and T37

One of the more interesting early post-war designs was the T28, which incorporated features from captured German *Sturmgewehre* (assault rifles). These included the roller locking system later to be used in the G3 rifle, and stampings. Designed by Cyril Moore and chambered for the improved version of the T65 cartridge, the T65E1, this rifle weighed only 6.9lb and was optimistically intended to replace the M1 rifle, M2 carbine, M3A1 SMG, and BAR. Various factors resulted in the cancellation of the project in late 1950 after comparison trials involving various other rifles, which will be discussed below (Stevens 1995: 104–06).

A soldier – who appears to be from the 101st Airborne Division, since he wears parachute wings on his left breast and an 101st Airborne Recondo (short for "Reconnaissance Commando") patch on his right pocket – holds the M14 rifle next to a table containing the weapons it was intended to replace: M3A1 SMG, M1 carbine, M1 rifle, and BAR. (NARA)

The T31 rifle was also intended to replace the rifle, carbine, SMG, and SAWs in use after World War II. A bullpup design that weighed 8.75lb, the T31 was intended to reduce recoil and muzzle flash, but did not succeed. This was the last rifle designed by John Garand. Its gas system used a full-length cylinder that surrounded the barrel and was similar to the gas-trap system used on early Garands. Chambering was for the T65E3 cartridge. Probably the most noteworthy feature of the T31 in the development history of the M14 rifle is its magazine, which would become the basis for that later adopted for the M14.

Other designs from the 1949–50 period included: the T33, which proved unsatisfactory due to its lack of durability under field conditions; the T34, which was the M1918A2 BAR chambered for the T65E3 cartridge (basically the future 7.62×51mm NATO round); and the T35, which was an M1 Garand chambered for the T65E3 cartridge. A T36 rifle, which was a modified T20E2 rifle chambered for the T65E3 cartridge and firing in full- or semiautomatic modes from a closed bolt and taking a T25 magazine, was also tested, as was the T37, basically a T36 with a straight-line stock of the type used on the T25 (Johnston & Nelson 2010: 966–67). The lightweight T37 weighed only 8.25lb and had a 22in barrel. It also included a lightweight stabilizer/flash hider and a bolt buffer to prevent over travel. This design was deemed worthy of further development (Iannamico 2005: 35–36), and led to the first of the T44 series of rifles.

The T44 versus the T48

With development of the T44, which used the T20E2 receiver, the M14 rifle began to take shape. Remington Arms had agreed to manufacture 30 test versions of the T44. Upon examining and testing the T44, Springfield Armory described it as follows:

> The rifle, Cal. 30, T44 is a modified design of the T20E2 Rifle for light weight and is capable of either full or semiautomatic fire, selectively, having many components common to the rifles, M1 and T20E2. It is gas operated, 43 inches long overall, and weighs 8 ¼ lbs. basically.

Right- and left-side views of the T47, which did not last past the 1952 trials. (Courtesy Collector Grade Publications, Inc.)

The subject rifle is furnished with a 20-round box magazine which is inserted in the bottom of the receiver. The combination stabilizer-flash suppressor on which the front sight is mounted is screwed onto the muzzle end of the barrel. The bayonet or grenade launcher may be attached to the suppressor.

Briefly, operational power is derived from a "gas cutoff and expansion system." In this system a metered quantity of gas is bled from the barrel and trapped in the gas cylinder. It is then allowed to expand, providing a power stroke during the expansion. The advantages of this actuating system lie in the fact that the applied power may be regulated as to magnitude, duration, and rate of application. (Quoted in Stevens 1995: 152)

Rifle trials were held between August 22 and December 29, 1952. Rifles in the trials included the "Rifle, Caliber .30, Lightweight, FN" (also known as the T48, but better known as the FN FAL), T47 (a much improved version of the T25), British EM-2 rifle (AKA Rifle No. 9 Mk 1), and Remington's T44, plus the M1 Garand as a control. This trial resulted in the FN being rated the winner by the Trials Board, with the T44 second, and the M1 Garand third. The T47 and British EM-2 were not rated highly enough to continue in further trials (Stevens 1995: 156). Among many US officers there was opposition to the adoption of a select-fire rifle on the basis that soldiers would waste ammunition, though it was agreed that there was a need for a SAW such as the BAR.

A demonstration of the T48, which was in competition with the T44E4 as the choice of the new US rifle. (NARA)

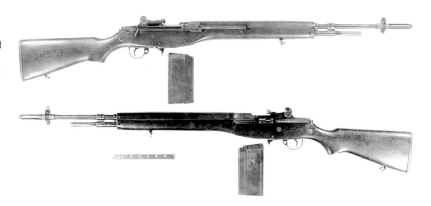

Right- and left-side views of the T44, which was manufactured at Springfield Armory using modified M1 Garand receivers. (Courtesy Collector Grade Publications, Inc.)

The T44E4 would receive the designation M14 for the standard rifle and M15 for the heavy-barreled SAW version. Here it is shown with its detachable 20-round box magazine removed. A high-capacity detachable magazine was one of the primary requirements for the new rifle. (NRA Museums, NRAmuseums.com)

The Trials Board did note that the T44 was more durable and reliable than the M1. Additionally, they felt that the T44 served well for use in close combat with the bayonet and noted that it weighed slightly over 1.5lb less than the M1. However, they still felt it was too heavy to replace the M2 carbine, and was much longer than the M3A1 SMG. At a March 1953 meeting of senior Ordnance officers at the Pentagon, an attempt was made to agree on alterations to the T44 to meet recommendations of the Trials Board, including eliminating the detachable magazine and limiting the rifle to semiautomatic fire. As a result, some T44 rifles were altered to take a ten-round magazine that could only be removed by stripping the rifle and were capable solely of semiautomatic fire. A T44E1 version had a heavier barrel and device to reduce the cyclic rate to a more controllable 350–400rds/min. This rifle was equipped with the John Garand-designed 20-round magazine from the T31, a bipod, and a butt plate, which could be folded up to rest atop the shoulder as an aid in controlling the rifle during full-automatic fire. The T44 and the T44E1 allowed loading of the magazine using five-round stripper clips. It appears that the semiautomatic T44 with fixed magazine was being tested to replace the M1 Garand and the T44E1 tested to replace the BAR.

A new series of tests was carried out in June 1953 at Fort Benning, Georgia. Although the T44/T44E1 performed better than previously, it still had more malfunctions than the T48. As a result of the tests, the Fort Benning Trials Board recommended that the T48 be adopted instead of the T44. In fact, the US Army Ordnance Corps ordered 3,000 FN rifles for further testing. However, it was decided by the Ordnance Corps to allow Springfield Armory to prepare T44 rifles for Arctic trials to take place from December 1953 through February 1954 at Big Delta, Alaska.

Among the modifications which took place were: redesign of the T31 magazine feed lips; addition of a stock liner for greater strength when firing grenades; installation of a gas plug with automatic bleed valve; and redesign of spring strengths and gas-port diameter for more effective operation in cold weather (Emerson 2010). The Arctic trials saved the T44, as the T48 did not function well in extreme cold. FN representatives enlarged the T48's gas port to increase reliability, but this caused a substantial increase in recoil and stress, causing parts to break. Although the T44 also had some problems with its gas valve, it outperformed the T48 to the extent that it got another chance to compete against it.

Previously, the T44 had been using receivers that had not been designed for what had now been adopted as the 7.62×51mm NATO round. For the T44E4, which would be submitted for the next trials, it was decided to fabricate a receiver around the new cartridge. However, Springfield Armory would take up to two years to design and fabricate the new receiver. To speed delivery for the next trials, Dave Mathewson, who ran a custom tool-and-die shop, was commissioned to build the prototype receivers in consultation with John Garand. The contract called for the first of 12 rifles to be ready by June 1, 1954 (Stevens 1995: 165). The rifle with the Mathewson receiver was designated the T44E4 and given a series of tests at Springfield Armory, including high-speed photography of the operating rod to determine most efficient rod functioning and of the bolt and operating-cam surfaces to determine most efficient operation. Functioning was tested with varying amounts of lubrication and in cold as well as dusty conditions. Simultaneously, efforts

A top view of the T44E4 showing the adjustable rear sight and the selector switch for full- or semiautomatic fire. (NRA Museums, NRAmuseums.com)

were under way to produce drawings in inch rather than metric dimensions for the T48. Additional Arctic trials were scheduled for the winter of 1954/55 but were delayed while awaiting US-made prototypes of the T48 from the High Standard Manufacturing Company Inc. To allow High Standard to produce the rifles using US customary standard tools and machinery, Canada, which had adopted the FAL, assisted with inch dimension drawings for the T48 (Iannamico 2005: 55).

When the Arctic trials actually got started at Fort Greely, Alaska, the T44E4 performed quite well. Further tests during the winter of 1954/55 at Fort Benning, Georgia, saw the T44E4 outperform the T48 – again due to the T48's close tolerances, which made it malfunction in dusty conditions. Longitudinal grooves machined into the T48's bolt carriers to allow sand or dirt to be carried away seemed to solve the problem, which the British had also encountered during sand testing (Iannamico 2005: 59). Another aspect of these tests was to determine optimal barrel length, with rifle barrels being fired to test center-of-impact stability, then shortened in .125in increments and fired again (Iannamico 2005: 45).

During this period, Springfield Armory had been working on the production of 500 T44E4 rifles, while The Harrington & Richardson Arms Company Incorporated (hereafter H&R) had been working on the production of 500 T48 rifles. H&R was, however, having problems with extraction and feeding. At Springfield Armory, methods to decrease the number of parts were being studied. For example, eight components of the gas cylinder and valve assembly were replaced with four simpler parts. However, Springfield Armory also suffered some delays due to changes in design and the limited number of personnel assigned to the project (Iannamico 2005: 45–46). Meanwhile, deliveries of the rifles from the order of 3,000 given to FN began. An additional 200 heavy-barreled FALs were ordered for testing as SAWs.

Testing of the T44E4 and T48 was scheduled to begin in September 1954, with expectations that a new US military rifle would emerge from the trials. There were, however, various delays to the testing, including a change in ammunition from the T104E1 round to the T104E2 round. About 10 grains (.065g) heavier than the T104E1 and featuring a slightly different ogive (curve of bullet's tip), the T104E2 is closer to the round that became the NATO standard 7.62×51mm load. Problems with magazine functioning for the T44E4 arose, but were corrected with a new magazine spring. Throughout the winter and spring of 1955, Springfield Armory continued to tweak the design of the T44E4. Delivery of the rifles was delayed by numerous revisions to drawings and 101 engineering changes, in some cases requiring parts on already completed rifles to be changed out (Iannamico 2005: 47). By October 1955, the rifles were completed and ready for shipment to various testing bodies.

In a test at Fort Benning during the fall of 1955, rifles were evaluated on a combat course, mostly for functioning and reliability. The T44E4 rifles malfunctioned 1.4 percent of the time, while the T48 rifles malfunctioned 2.4 percent of the time (Stevens 1995: 174). Both Springfield Armory and H&R worked on improving their test guns, with the H&R T48s being ready by December 1955. Trials of the production samples began once again at Aberdeen Proving Ground, but the H&R T48s could not meet the qualifying accuracy standards. It turned out that to allow the broaches used to rifle the T48 barrels to last longer, they had been made at the top of the allowable dimensions; this, combined with an incorrect upper tolerance on the barrels, resulted in oversized, inaccurate barrels (Stevens 1995: 174).

It had been planned that final testing of the T44E4, T48, and FN-produced FAL would take place beginning in April 1956. The trials as intended never took place, but a compressed series of trials were run at the Fort Benning Combat Course and the USMC Test Center at Quantico, Virginia, over a period of months during 1956. Late in that year, Aberdeen Proving Ground submitted a report, which concluded that the latest versions of the T44E4 and the T48 were suitable for Army use. At the Pentagon, the preference was for the T44E4, which was of US design and retained many of the features of the familiar M1 Garand. Additionally, the T44E4 had fewer parts, used a gas-flow system requiring no manual adjustments, and was lighter than the T48 by about 1lb. Wilber H. Brucker, the Secretary of the Army, announced the adoption of the new rifles on May 1, 1957 (Stevens 1995: 176). It had taken more than a decade of development at a cost of over $100 million (Iannamico 2005: 65).

The original intent had been for the M14 and M15 to replace an array of other infantry weapons, but this would have required making variants of the M14, such as a model with shorter barrel and folding stock to replace the M2 carbine and M3A1 SMG. Other than in prototype form, however, the M14 "carbine" was never produced. Neither was the M15 in any numbers. Instead, a new general-purpose machine gun, the M60, was introduced in 1957 chambered for the same 7.62×51mm NATO round as the M14.

In evaluating the various trials that resulted in the adoption of the M14 rifle, it is worthwhile to consider the comments of Edward Ezell – a distinguished figure in the study of the history and present-day use of small arms – on testing of a new weapon:

An Ordnance Department illustration of the new M14 rifle. Edward Ezell offers a very pointed evaluation of the shortcomings of the Ordnance Corps, which would lead to many of the problems with the M14 program: "It is a toss-up as to which element of the Ordnance Corps was most responsible for the production problems. The Ordnance Technical Committee, Ordnance Weapons Command, and Headquarters of the Ordnance Corps all demonstrated a remarkable absence of initiative and thought. The Ordnance Technical Committee contributed to its share of the problems of procuring the new rifle through insufficient planning prior to the decision about which rifle would be adopted. Weapons Command personnel added to the problems when they held up the pre-production engineering studies for the M14 rifle. Headquarters, Ordnance Corps, abdicated its responsibilities for overseeing the project until the production crisis of 1960–61 forced its personnel to act. Taken together, the inaction of these three organizations led to unnecessary troubles" (Ezell 1984: 139–40). (NARA)

The flip-up butt plate of the M14 was designed to grant better control and to counter muzzle climb during full-automatic fire; note the access panel to the recess in the butt for cleaning tools. (Author)

Test [*sic*] of a new weapon can have several effects. They can be used to assist in the selection of a new rifle. They can also delay or prevent change. Testing schedules can be so established that they hamper the development of the item in question. Under such circumstances the engineer has to adjust his development schedule to meet the demands of the officers judging the rifles. Just the opposite should be the case. Furthermore, even though the tests are objective and honest in their design, they can be made to serve political purposes. The testing process is not always as simple and straightforward as it might appear on the surface. (Ezell 1984: 108)

Various elements mentioned by Ezell are apparent in the testing procedure for the M14. Pressure from other NATO members to adopt the FAL was a factor, as were those elements of the US armed forces that wanted a lighter rifle chambered for a smaller cartridge. Another aspect was the US insistence on the adoption of the 7.62×51mm cartridge as NATO standard. In any case, the M14 was now adopted and ready for production.

INTO PRODUCTION

A troubled start

Since the M14 was adopted after the end of the Korean War and before the beginning of the Vietnam War, despite the specter of the Cold War, there was no rush to produce the M14 in large numbers. Prior to receiving its first order for M14 production, Springfield Armory received an order to prepare the Technical Data Package (TDP) for the M14 to include drawings, gauges, and production schedules. These preparations were deemed an extremely important step in opening the M14 up to competitive bidding by other contractors. However, Springfield Armory was ordered to rush preparation of the TDP and to limit data on changes with which they had been experimenting (Stevens 1995: 198).

In April 1958, Springfield Armory received an order for pilot production of the M14 totaling 15,669 rifles – in actuality, 15,600 production rifles and 69 for additional testing (Stevens 1995: 198). Once Springfield Armory began production, it was determined that using the

> **Shipping the M14**
>
> Before the troops could be issued the M14, it had to be shipped to them. Springfield Armory had undertaken a study to determine the least expensive yet effective method for shipping the rifle. It concluded that two rifles should be wrapped in a single sheet of VCI (Volatile Corrosion Inhibitor) paper, then packaged in a carton with cardboard end blocks and a separator so the weapons would not move around. Nylon tape was then used to seal the cartons. A total of 225 two-rifle cartons were packed in a Conex container, which had been brought to the proper humidity level prior to inserting packing and desiccant, after which the container was sealed (Iannamico 2005: 99).

procedures it had developed, it would take 10.4 direct labor hours to produce each M14 rifle (Iannamico 2005: 72). Owing to reductions in personnel, at this point Springfield Armory only had the capacity to produce 2,000 rifles a month. Nevertheless, the US Air Force (hereafter USAF) foresaw the purchase of 2 million M14s and the Army 5 million over the next few years (Johnston & Nelson 2010: 973). These figures would prove very optimistic, especially since the USAF chose to retain its M2 carbines and would soon focus on the AR-15 rifle.

To expand production, on February 17, 1959, Winchester was given a contract to produce 35,000 M14s, deliveries to begin within a year. Winchester's bid was at a price of $69.75 per rifle (Stevens 1995: 200). As Winchester had produced the M1 Garand during World War II it was considered that the company should have gained some experience that would be useful in producing the M14. A second contract was awarded, to H&R in April 1959 for 35,000 rifles. H&R also had experience in producing the M1 Garand, having manufactured it in 1953–56. Additional contracts were awarded to H&R in February 1960, for 70,000 rifles, and to Winchester in April 1960, for 81,500 rifles. Production was slow, however, as by June 1960, only 9,471 rifles were available from all sources (Johnston & Nelson 2010: 974). In part, this delay was due to a steel strike in 1959, which delayed deliveries of special steels needed for production of the rifles. An unintended consequence for the United Steel Workers was that this strike led to the large-scale importation of foreign steel, which would drastically impact the US steel industry in the future.

Fort Myer, Virginia, December 19, 1961: One of a sequence of photographs showing a demonstration of the new M14 rifle by Private First Class Kenneth Long of the 3rd Infantry Division. (NARA)

THE M14 EXPOSED

7.62×51mm M14 rifle

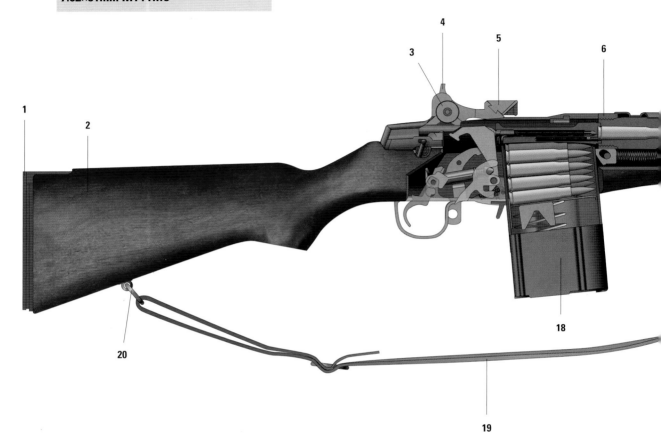

1.	Butt-plate assembly	**14.**	Gas cylinder	**27.**	Cartridge in chamber
2.	Buttstock	**15.**	Gas piston	**28.**	Barrel
3.	Rear sight elevation knob	**16.**	Lower gas port	**29.**	Operating-rod spring
4.	Rear aperture sight	**17.**	Forward sling swivel	**30.**	Operating-rod spring guide
5.	Cartridge clip guide	**18.**	Magazine	**31.**	Magazine-follower spring
6.	Receiver	**19.**	Sling	**32.**	Magazine-follower plate
7.	Handguard	**20.**	Rear sling swivel	**33.**	Magazine latch
8.	Operating rod	**21.**	Hammer-spring housing	**34.**	Magazine-latch spring
9.	Gas port	**22.**	Hammer plunger	**35.**	Trigger guard
10.	Bullet	**23.**	Hammer	**36.**	Safety
11.	Front sight	**24.**	Ejector spring	**37.**	Trigger
12.	Flash suppressor	**25.**	Firing pin		
13.	Gas cylinder plug	**26.**	Bolt		

Improvements and setbacks

Early in 1960 the decision was made to fit future production M14s with a ventilated plastic handguard, flip-up-style butt plate, and the M2 bipod. These were features that had been incorporated into the M15 rifle intended as a SAW. Rifles already produced were to be retrofitted with the changes at New Jersey's Raritan Arsenal (Iannamico 2005: 74). During its early production, Springfield Armory had also determined that the cast flash suppressor could be replaced by a forged one that was of higher quality at less than half the cost (Iannamico 2005: 78–79). Other parts were simplified during early production at Springfield Armory, with the information passed on to the commercial contractors.

Production was slowed even more in December 1960, when receivers and bolts of H&R M14s being tested at Fort Benning fractured. As a result, the Chief of Ordnance halted production at both Winchester and H&R for two months while a team of engineers from Springfield Armory assessed the problem. It was determined that some incoming steel had been of the wrong type for use in receivers, resulting in brittleness when heat-treated. Some receivers had fractured, while some bolts had broken at the locking lugs due to improper heat treatment. As a result, before production resumed, the Ordnance Weapons Command instituted Engineering Order No. 164, stipulating a much more stringent heat-treatment and inspection procedure at both contractors. Springfield Armory received a contract for an additional 70,500 M14 rifles in March 1961, as quality control at the Armory was not in doubt (Stevens 1995: 201–02). Nevertheless, random testing of bolts was required at all three manufacturers.

In an attempt to increase production of the M14 and quickly deal with any new problems that arose, General Elmer J. Gibson, the Commanding General of Ordnance Weapons Command at Rock Island Arsenal, became the project manager of the M14 program. One solution to the production problem was to solicit another commercial producer of the M14. To encourage timely production, the contract for the new vender would include an incentive for each rifle delivered early (Stevens 1995: 202). A total of 42 firms applied in March 1961 to bid on the new contract. Among the bidders were some very well-known companies such as: Chrysler Corporation, Colt Industries, Curtiss-Wright Corporation, Ford Motor Company, General Dynamics, Ithaca Gun Company, Remington Arms Corporation, Studebaker-Packard, and Westinghouse Electric among others. Also bidding was ArmaLite Incorporated of Costa Mesa, California, the developer of the AR-15 rifle, which would replace the M14 within a decade (Stevens 1995: 203).

There was little doubt that production needed to be increased at Springfield Armory, H&R, and Winchester, as by June 30, 1961, a total of only 133,386 M14 rifles had been produced (Stevens 1995: 204). Needless to say, members of Congress were not happy that US troops in Europe facing the Berlin Crisis of June 4–November 9, 1961 were still armed with the M1 Garand (Stevens 1995: 205). Although not necessarily stated within the US armed forces, the specter of two 7.62×39mm weapons in the hands of Soviet and other troops – the SKS semiautomatic

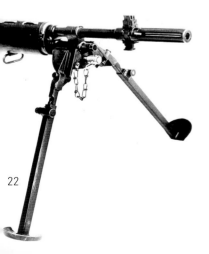

A US Army Infantry Board illustration of the M15's bipod modified for use on the M14 when serving as a SAW. (NARA)

carbine and, especially, the AK-47 assault rifle – added impetus to the need to get M14s into the hands of US troops. These Soviet weapons would give the United States' enemies rifles that had the advantages of the Garand but were lighter and more user-friendly; and the AK-47 had a high-capacity detachable box magazine and full-auto capability.

October 1961 saw the publication of an article on the M14 in *The American Rifleman*, the most influential arms magazine in the USA. With full cooperation of the US Army Ordnance Corps, staff members of the magazine visited the manufacturers of the M14 and interviewed government officials as well as management at the production facilities. As an interesting sidebar to the article, *The American Rifleman* summarized the teething problems of the M1 Garand when it was adopted in order to put into perspective early problems with the M14. It is noted in the article that Winchester had experience in manufacturing the M1 Garand during World War II and H&R in manufacturing it during the Korean War. The article also notes that the $68.75 price negotiated for the rifles was quite low, but that the two arms companies were desperate to keep their skilled employees working. The writers speculate, though, that this low price may have led to cutting corners during production. The price was eventually negotiated upwards to $95.00 (Howe & Harrison 1961: 19).

During April 1958, a demonstration of the "Rifle, Cal .30, T44, Grenade Launching M29 (T42)," a training practice round. (NARA)

Owing to the sophistication of *The American Rifleman*'s readers in matters related to arms and their production, the article's authors, Walter J. Howe and E.H. Harrison, go into quite a bit of detail about the problems H&R and Winchester encountered, including those related to heat treatment already discussed above. For example, it is pointed out that the steel Winchester was required to use for barrels was extremely difficult to machine, while Springfield Armory and H&R were allowed to use another steel that was within specifications but easier to machine. Winchester's difficulties in receiving permission from the Ordnance Department to use the easier-to-machine steel contributed to their slowness of production (Howe & Harrison 1961: 21). It should be pointed out, however, that Springfield Armory and H&R were both using the broaching process to rifle the barrel, which entailed the use of a toothed rotary tool that was placed inside the barrel and rotated and pulled through, while Winchester milled its barrels, which entailed cutting one groove at a time with a machine tool. Broaching was a faster process.

By the time the National Rifle Association (NRA) team visited the three M14 producers, most problems had been solved and production was increasing, in part due to the use of new machinery capable of performing multiple operations. Winchester was on track to produce 10,000 rifles per month by the end of 1961 and H&R to deliver 16,000 per month. Springfield Armory could produce more but because of other responsibilities was building only 6,500 per month. It should be borne in mind that Springfield Armory was intended to be a primary producer of the M14. Instead, the Armory was to set up a pilot production line to work out the bugs of production and to act as a technical source for commercial producers of the rifle (Iannamico 2005: 69). As of the publication of the article, H&R had orders for 238,000 rifles to be completed by May 1962, Winchester for 116,500 rifles to be completed by July 1962, and Springfield Armory for 118,100 rifles to be completed by May 1962, for a total of 472,600 rifles. These figures include third orders for H&R, while Winchester had its initial two orders (Howe & Harrison 1961: 24). H&R's acceptance procedure, as described in the article, offers an insight into the quality-control program for the M14:

> Every rifle, after a high-pressure proof round, must successfully pass a functioning test of semiautomatic, burst automatic, and sustained automatic fire, and its speed in automatic fire must be within narrow limits. It must deliver its center of impact within a certain limited area around point of aim at 100 yds. with rear sight set 8 clicks up from zero elevation, and zero windage. It must make 5-shot groups within 5.6" at 100 yds. with Service, not Match, ammunition (the present average of all rifles is about half that). There are 5% to 12% of failures from all causes, all producers considered. Rifles which fail are returned to manufacturer tagged to show the failure and the parts apparently involved. After replacement of parts and re-inspection, most rifles pass second firing test. Information on the tags is transferred to records which are analyzed to detect manufacturing processes needing attention. (Howe & Harrison 1961: 27)

The article summarizes the impressions of the NRA team as follows: "The NRA team completed its plant visits with an extremely favorable impression of all 3 producers. Their spirit is something exceptional. The size and quality of their operation arouses real admiration. The contractors undoubtedly had serious problems, but it is evident that in the main they have overcome them, and the present production rate speaks for itself" (Howe & Harrison 1961: 24). As mentioned above, the Ordnance Department determined that a third manufacturer of the M14 was needed, which resulted in the award of a contract for 100,000 rifles to Thompson-Ramo-Wooldridge, Inc. (TRW) on October 2, 1961. Rifles were to be produced at a cost of $85.54 each to the government, which agreed to assist in remodeling TRW's plant at Cleveland, Ohio, into an "Ordnance Works" capable of producing the rifle (Stevens 1995: 221).

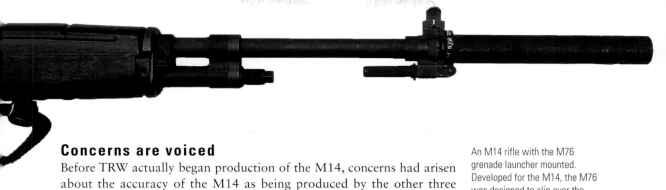

Concerns are voiced

Before TRW actually began production of the M14, concerns had arisen about the accuracy of the M14 as being produced by the other three manufacturers. The USMC, always an advocate of rifle marksmanship, had raised concerns as had others. An Aberdeen Proving Ground report of March 1962 concluded that the problem lay in the accuracy test standards for the rifle combined with the accuracy standards in the specifications for US military 7.62×51mm ammunition. To summarize as concisely as possible, the criteria for accepting cartridges for accuracy was arithmetic average of distance between the center of each bullet hole and the center of impact based on the geometric center of the group around the point of aim. Accuracy of the rifle was tested based on the size of a five-shot group (Stevens 1995: 225–26).

The Boston Ordnance District, which had been in charge of final acceptance for rifles produced by H&R and Winchester, had carried out tests that helped define the problem. The report is quite technical but points out that ammunition accuracy tests were carried out using heavy-barreled rifles with special slides, mounts, and accessories. Generally, however, tests showed that the ammunition being produced met accuracy standards. Tests of 21 rifles, seven pulled from production at each of three manufacturers, showed substantial faults with the rifles themselves that affected accuracy. Among the problems identified by L.F. Moore, a civilian test engineer at Aberdeen Proving Ground, in the rifles randomly selected were: head spaces that exceeded the standard; bore dimensions that exceeded the maximum; variations of bore diameter at various points in the length of the bore; trigger pulls with excessive creep; chromium plating of barrels under specified thickness; looseness of various parts; rear sights which could not be adjusted fully; and chambers that had a rough finish. It was determined in test firing that some bullets were hitting the flash suppressor, thus deflecting their path. It was also determined that even flash suppressors properly installed adversely affected accuracy as did the M14's gas system, which caused variations in gas pressure that affected barrel harmonics (Stevens 1995: 234–36). Recommendations included better quality-control inspections of the rifles and continued study of "the relationship between the dispersion contributed by the rifle and that contributed by the ammunition" (quoted in Stevens 1995: 236).

An M14 rifle with the M76 grenade launcher mounted. Developed for the M14, the M76 was designed to slip over the M14's rather long flash suppressor, and then secured by a latch that fit over the bayonet lug. Since the M14 had an adjustable gas valve, gas flow could be shut off to allow launching grenades with the M64 grenade-launching projectile, then turned back on when ready to fire on full- or semiautomatic. This was a real advantage over the Garand, which did not have an adjustable gas system. Distance of travel for the grenade could be determined by sliding the grenade to a specific one of the nine grooves on the M76 grenade launcher. Using the M64 grenade-launching projectile, a grenade could be launched to 250m (273yd). (John Miller)

An M14 rifle with M76 grenade launcher and an M31 HEAT (high-explosive anti-tank) grenade mounted. The same grenade-launcher sight used with the M1 Garand, the M15, was used with the M14 rifle. Development of the M79 grenade launcher and later the M203 grenade launcher would make the rifle-mounted grenade launcher obsolete by the late 1960s. (John Miller)

A close-up of the M14 flash suppressor and bayonet lug. (Author)

In a follow-up article to their previous examination of the M14 program for *The American Rifleman*, Howe and Harrison visited TRW for the February 1963 issue. This article notes that TRW was awarded the contract on October 2, 1961, and given until November 1962 to begin deliveries of completed rifles. An additional contract was awarded to TRW for $6,522,164 to allow upgrading of facilities and purchasing production equipment, which would lower the production cost of each rifle. TRW would receive another contract on October 9, 1962 for an additional 219,691 M14 rifles at $79.45 per rifle. This article also lists total orders for M14 rifles from each manufacturer as of 1963 as follows: Springfield Armory 167,100, H&R 537,582, Winchester 356,501, and TRW 319,391. With three commercial manufacturers producing the rifle, it was planned that Springfield Armory production would be phased out by September 1963 (Howe & Harrison 1963: 18).

TRW had been involved in the manufacture of automotive, electro-mechanical, electronics, and space technology. At the time, TRW was the largest supplier of jet engine components for the aircraft industry (Howe & Harrison 1963: 15). TRW's background in producing precision materials weighed heavily in the Ordnance Weapons Command's decision to grant the company the M14 contract despite the fact that TRW had no prior experience in weapons production. In fact, the lack of previous weapons experience proved an advantage as TRW engineers evaluated the sample M14 rifles they received and developed production procedures not based on any preconceptions (Howe & Harrison 1963: 19). For example, TRW would use continuous chain broaching in producing the M14 rifle. This process, which was common in producing jet-engine parts, allows more surfaces to be machined with one pass than with conventional broaching. TRW also employed a lateral-transfer machine to perform 30 operations on two M14 bolts clamped to a pallet, thus allowing this one-man machine to replace 15 machines that would have been required using single-point machining. TRW even applied its high-tech approach to range

National Match M14s

An interesting aspect of TRW production of the M14 rifle is that in January 1964, the Army Weapons Command announced that TRW would be producing National Match M14 rifles with some assistance from Springfield Armory, which had previously produced all National Match weapons. Ironically, by this time, TRW's M14 contract had been cancelled, late in 1963 (Iannamico 2005: 104). TRW would produce 4,874 of the total of 18,325 National Match M14s. During 1962, Springfield Armory had built 3,000 National Match rifles and during 1963, Springfield Armory built another 3,500. After 1964, National Match rifles were not built as new production but were rebuilt rifles, with Springfield producing 2,094 in 1965 and 2,395 in 1966, and Rock Island Arsenal building 2,462 in 1967 (Poyer 2000: 10). Some additional National Match rifles were also built by USAF, US Navy, or USMC armorers for competitors from those branches of the service.

Development of the National Match version of the M14 began in 1959, though the first rifles weren't built until 1962 when the M14 replaced the M1 as the official US National Match rifle. Lessons learned in building Match versions of the M1 Garand helped in developing the M14 National Match rifle. Features of the National Match M14 included: a bore held to half the tolerance of the service rifle and not chromed; the receiver fiberglass bedded into the stock; barrels not in contact with the stock; critical internal parts hand fitted and assembled; trigger free from creep and adjusted to break at 4.5lb–6lb; an improved rear sight that allowed adjustments in ½ MOA (minute of angle) clicks instead of 1 MOA on the service rifle; flash suppressor fastened securely to the barrel; and parts related to full-auto fire were welded so that the rifle could only fire in semiautomatic mode.

In *The M14 Owner's Guide*, Scott Duff points out that each National Match M14 was required to fire 62 rounds without malfunction. Accuracy requirements stipulated an extreme spread of six ten-shot groups averaging 3.5in at 100yd (91m); this was modified in the 1970s to five ten-shot groups (Duff & Miller 2001: 12). The firing of 62 rounds for reliability was actually combined with the accuracy test. Rounds were fired from a "jack" – a mechanical rifle rest – with the two extra rounds required to check the rifle's retention in the jack/rack and front-sight alignment. Note that firing a tight ten-shot group is much more difficult than firing a tight three- or five-shot group, because each round fired offers more chance of spreading the group through slight differences in bullet powder, etc., even when fired from a rest.

Unlike previous National Match rifles, M14 versions could not be sold to civilian shooters due to the fact they were originally produced as full-automatic weapons. Some of the semiautomatic National Match rifles were signed out under strict controls to competitors for state rifle teams.

March 16, 1965: In an obvious attempt to link the M14 with the US tradition of military marksmanship, Private James H. York, the nephew of famous World War I Medal of Honor Sergeant Alvin C. York, holds an M14 at Fort Gordon, Georgia. (NARA)

testing the rifles, as closed-circuit cameras allowed the test firer to review shooting results rapidly, and targets could be changed quickly by push-button controls (Stevens 1995: 224). Ironically, however, even through the 1963 article lauds TRW's use of modern production techniques and the fact that the M14 program was running smoothly at the three civilian contractors, it also points out that the USAF had already expressed an interest in adopting the ArmaLite AR-15 rifle, the weapon which would eventually supplant the M14 (Howe & Harrison 1963: 20).

Procurement is terminated

Based on various tests, which some argued were biased in favor of the AR-15 rifle, on January 23, 1963, Defense Secretary Robert McNamara announced that at the end of that fiscal year procurement of the M14

With some units, the M14 remained in use into the 1970s. This Marine is taking part in a joint US Army/USMC exercise at Camp A.P. Hill, Virginia, during October 1976. It is possible that he is a Marine reservist. (NARA)

would be terminated. It should be pointed out also that in testing of the AR-15 for the USAF at Aberdeen Proving Ground on September 26, 1960, the AR-15 had clearly outperformed the M14 (Hallahan 1994: 469). He also announced that 85,000 AR-15s would be purchased for the Army and 19,000 for the USAF (Stevens 1995: 241). Total production of the M14 rifle from all sources was as follows: Springfield Armory 167,100; Winchester-Western 356,501; H&R 537,582; and TRW 319,163. Total production came to 1,380,346 (Johnston & Nelson 2010: 976). Springfield Armory was the first to cease production of the M14, by September 1963. The other three manufacturers finished their production during the early months of 1964 (Stevens 1995: 244). However, the NATO agreement standardizing the 7.62×51mm cartridge was not up for renewal until January 1, 1968. As a result, the M14 would be classified "Standard A" until at least that date even though AR-15/M16 rifles were being widely issued in Southeast Asia by 1966 (Stevens 1995: 247). The M14 would remain standard issue among troops assigned to NATO for at least a few years.

The T44E5, the select-fire, heavy-barreled version of the T44 adopted as the M15 in May 1957. (Courtesy Collector Grade Publications, Inc.)

M14 VARIANTS

The M14E1

There was an attempt to develop a folding-stock M14 for airborne troops as well as tankers and drivers. This rifle, designated the M14E1, did not make it past prototype stage due to the ending of M14 production. Four variations of stock were developed during 1962, including side-folding and under-folding, one of which was very similar to that used on the Soviet AKM. The most complicated, labeled the Type IV, was side-folding and incorporated folding rear and forward pistol grips. A Type V side-folder was offered in two versions, one with a sliding folding foregrip and folding rear grip as well as a thicker butt plate for use in full-automatic mode as a SAW, and one with folding stock and folding rear pistol grip for use as a semiautomatic rifle (Stevens 1995: 252–56).

February 1963: This photograph shows a member of the 101st Airborne Division with an M14 modified for airborne troops through the installation of an aluminum stock with pistol grip. (NARA)

The M14E2/M14A1

Most often cited as the primary problems with the M14 were the following: difficulty of control in full-automatic mode; inherent inaccuracy; and lack of a folding stock model for airborne or other specialized troops. Prior to and during the phasing out of the M14, some attempts had been made to address these problems. An especially sensitive issue was controlling the M14 during full-automatic fire. Some aspects of the defunct M15 – the hinged hook butt plate, M2 bipod, and vented fiberglass handguard – had been added to M14s intended to function as a SAW, but full-automatic performance was only improved marginally. In 1959, Captain Durward Dean Gosney, who was serving as a technical advisor on weapons to the Infantry Board during evaluation of the M14 rifle, developed some ideas to enhance controllability of the M14 through redesign of the stock. These included an in-line stock that would align the centerline of the barrel with the stock. Additionally, the stock would have a polymer rear pistol grip, a folding vertical foregrip, and a rubber recoil pad with hooked butt plate. Since the right-hand twist of the M14's barrel combined with bullet torque tended to pull the stock up and to the right during full-automatic fire, a muzzle brake that countered this tendency was also developed (Iannamico 2005: 175).

February 1965: A soldier fires an M14E2 (later M14A1) with infrared illuminator and sight. (NARA)

A prototype of an M14 incorporating Gosney's alterations was shipped to Springfield Armory in the spring of 1962 for evaluation. A positive report on its performance was sent from the Infantry Board to the US Ordnance Weapon Command. Springfield Armory was tasked with developing a production model of the rifle. Springfield Armory developed five prototype rifles that were shipped to the Infantry Board for evaluation in November 1963, while another eight with winter triggers were sent to the Arctic Board in Alaska for cold-weather tests. The test rifles received a favorable report on their improved accuracy in burst fire from those carrying out tests. There were some suggestions for additional improvements such as strengthening the muzzle stabilizer and stock where the foregrip was attached.

The M14A1 (previously M14E2) version of the M14 set up to function as a SAW. Note the pistol grip stock, bipod, and vertical foregrip. (John Miller)

These improvements were incorporated into what was now called the M14E2, with 8,350 M14 rifles to be converted to E2 configuration. Springfield Armory built the stocks, which were initially intended for shipment to Winchester and TRW for assembly as M14E2 rifles. However, due to delays, by the time the stocks were ready, Winchester and TRW were no longer producing the rifles (Iannamico 2005: 177–79). During 1964, Springfield Armory obtained 50 M14 rifles and assembled them with the E2 stocks for testing with the bipod. In June 1964, 224 M14E2 rifles were ordered from Springfield Armory for shipment to Southeast Asia; however, due to a delay in getting foregrips from the subcontractor, they were not shipped until July.

By December 1964, all 8,350 M14E2 rifles had been completed (Iannamico 2005: 180). As those rifles made it into the hands of troops, various problems arose, including: muzzle stabilizers coming off during firing; stocks breaking where the foregrip was attached; front handgrips breaking; and the M2 bipods working loose. Springfield Armory engineers redesigned these parts to be sturdier and also added a new synthetic rubber butt pad more resistant to cleaning solvents (Iannamico 2005: 180). After additional field trials, the improved version was eventually adopted as the M14A1 in April 1966. However, since the M14 was no longer in production, it was necessary to find a contractor to build the stocks. The contract was given to Canadian Arsenals Limited (Iannamico 2005: 185). It should be noted that friends of the author who were familiar with firing the M14A1 stated that it was prone to "cook offs" (a round firing due to excessive heat in the chamber resulting from the closed-bolt design) and the wooden handguard catching on fire.

USE
The M14 goes to war

INTO SERVICE

Reportedly, the first US Army unit fully equipped with the M14 was the 101st Airborne Division. By October 1, 1961, all US infantry units in Western Europe had been issued the M14. A *Rifle Evaluation Study* from the Infantry Combat Development Agency dated December 8, 1962, sets forth two infantry squad organizations for troops armed with the M14:

ROAD RIFLE SQUAD
TOE/-18E

Squad Leader	M-14, bayonet
Fire Team Leader	M-14, bayonet
Automatic Rifleman	M-14 w/bipod, bayonet
Grenadier	40mm Grenade Launcher, pistol
Rifleman	M-14, bayonet
Rifleman	M-14, bayonet
Fire Team Leader	M-14, bayonet
Automatic Rifleman	M-14 w/bipod, bayonet
Grenadier	40mm Grenade Launcher, pistol
Rifleman	M-14, bayonet

INFANTRY SQUAD PROPOSED BY FT BENNING AD HOC COMMITTEE

Each Rifle Platoon contains 3 rifle squads.

Squad Leader	M-14, bayonet
Asst. Squad Leader	M-14, bayonet
Machinegunner	M60 machinegun, pistol
Asst. Machinegunner	M-14, bayonet
Rifleman (ammo bearer)	M-14, bayonet

2 Grenadiers	M79, pistol
1 Automatic Rifleman	M-14, w/bipod, bayonet
3 Riflemen	M-14, bayonet
(US Army 1962b: 5)	

ROAD refers to the "Reorganization Objective Army Division," a reorganization of US Army divisions replacing the Pentomic Division – which had been designed to have a higher survival rate on the nuclear battlefield – with a 1960s division with similarities to those of World War II but more flexibility in organization. One development of the ROAD concept was the August 1962 recommendation to develop an airmobile division. For purposes of this work the most noteworthy difference in the organization of the two infantry squad models is the replacement of one of the automatic riflemen with an M60 machine-gunner, thus increasing the sustained-fire support capability of the squad. In Vietnam, the typical infantry company had six M60 general-purpose machine guns (GPMGs) and 24 M79 grenade launchers, which resulted in rifle platoons being armed with M16s and M79s with one weapons squad that had two M60s.

The Fleet Marine Force, the combination of US Navy ships and US Marines trained and structured to carry out offensive amphibious and expeditionary warfare, was another high-priority unit that had replaced its M1 Garands with M14s by the end of 1962. US Army units deployed to Vietnam early in the conflict – such as the 1st Infantry Division, deployed to Vietnam in July 1965 – were also armed with the M14. According to Lee Emerson and other sources, most M14 rifles in the Army were issued with the selector shaft locked so that they would only fire on semiautomatic. Within the USMC, however, the TO&E (table of

Germany, February 1969: While taking part in Operation *Reforger*, a soldier of the 32nd Armored Cavalry Regiment, 24th Infantry Division, takes time to disassemble and clean his M14 rifle. US troops assigned to Germany retained their M14s after the M16 became standard issue in Vietnam. An M60 machine gun, chambered for the same 7.62×51mm round as the M14, is leaning at the right. (NARA)

A member of the USMC 1st Recon Battalion prior to going on a patrol in Vietnam; he is armed with an M14 rifle as well as a Ka-Bar knife and M26 fragmentation grenades on his webbed gear. (NARA)

organization and equipment) specified three automatic riflemen per squad armed with select-fire M14s. This was partially a factor of USMC squad organization, as each squad had three four-man fire teams, each with one automatic rifleman. Some USMC units in Vietnam, such as the 1st Recon Battalion, would be entirely equipped with select-fire M14s. Presumably the higher likelihood that the Recon Marines would encounter enemy ambushes justified the additional firepower.

TRAINING WITH THE M14

US Army

Once the M14 rifle was issued to troops in Europe, South Korea, and – early in the Vietnam commitment – to US troops in Vietnam, it took some time before the M14 was available at the various basic training sites. As a result, recruits continued to be trained with the M1 Garand. Since the sights, safety, and some other elements of the M14 were very similar to those of the M1 Garand, transitioning to the M14 was not as difficult as it would be later, when the M14 was used in basic training but troops deploying to Vietnam were issued the M16. In fact, National Guard units continued to be issued M1 Garands until at least 1966 or later (Poyer 2000: 66).

Once troops were issued their M14 rifles, stress was put on learning to shoot them well. Included in training was learning to use the M14's rear sight. The sight is explained in *FM 23-8, M14 and M14A1 Rifles and Rifle Marksmanship* as follows:

The M14 uses the same safety system as the M1 Garand; the lever could be pushed into the trigger guard to put the rifle on safe (as shown) or pushed forward to put the rifle on fire. (Author)

47. Sights

a. The rear sight (fig. 80) of the M14 and M14A1 rifle has an elevation knob and a windage knob which are used to move the rear sight aperture up or down and right or left respectively. Changing the position of the rear sight aperture causes a corresponding change in the location of the strike of the bullet. The elevation knob affects the vertical location of the strike of the bullet, while the windage knob affects the horizontal location. Both knobs make an audible click when they are turned. Each click changes the strike of the bullet a specific distance, depending on the range to the target. The elevation knob is adjustable from 0 to 72 clicks. The rear sight aperture can be adjusted from 0 to 16 clicks to the right or left of the center index line by rotating the windage knob. (US Army 1974: 92)

March 1965: US Army trainees march with the M14 rifle at Fort Gordon, Georgia. (NARA)

Once the soldier understood how the sights were adjusted, he was taught to set his battlesight zero on a 25m (27yd) target using an aiming point on the target. By firing three-shot groups, the soldier would adjust his group until it was centered on a point 46mm (1.81in) above the point of aim, a point designated by an "X" on the target. This 25m battlesight zero will be very close to "on" – the term used to designate when the sights are on target – at 250m (273yd). Once he had found the battlesight zero, he would adjust the rear sight to calibrate it so that he could quickly change the elevation for other distances or return quickly to the battlesight zero position. Troops transitioning from the M1 Garand would have found this process quite similar to that used with the M1, though the battlesight zero with the M1 was 300yd (274m).

Despite the ability to load the M14 more quickly using the 20-round detachable box magazine, troops were still taught that the magazine could be left in place and reloaded using five-round stripper clips. It is also interesting to note that *Department of the Army Field Manual FM23-8* for the M14 rifle sets very conservative recommended rates of fire:

Rates of Fire. (These can be maintained without danger to the firer, or damage to the weapon):
Semiautomatic (rounds per minute)

1 minute	40
2 minutes	40
5 minutes	30
10 minutes	20
15 minutes	20
20 minutes	20
30 minutes (or more)	15

October 1966: A SEABEE (member of a US Navy Construction Battalion) receives instruction in firing his M14 from the sitting position at Camp Shelby, Mississippi. A point to note when training personnel to fire the M14 was the calibration of the rear sight. When the sight was marked with an "M" this indicated that the markings of 2, 4, 6, 8, 10, and 12 represented hundreds of meters; however, Garand sights which were not marked with an "M" had markings that represented yards. To adjust windage or elevation, one click of the dial moved point of impact 1in at 100m (109yd) on the standard M14 rifle. (NARA)

Automatic (rounds per minute)	
1 minute	60
2 minutes	50
5 minutes	40
10 minutes	30
15 minutes	30
20 minutes	25
30 minutes (or more)	20
(US Army 1965: 5)	

The manual does not give a justification for these rates of fire, but presumably they are intended to keep the weapon from overheating and to encourage aimed fire and ammunition conservation among troops issued the M14.

USMC

Once the M14 was issued to recruits in the USMC, in standard Corps fashion, it became part of the cadences chanted by the recruits as they ran: "I don't need no teenage queen, I just need my M14"; "See that commie dressed in red, put a 7.62 in his head." Within the first two or three weeks of boot camp, Marines were issued their M14 rifles, along with two magazines, magazine pouches, sling, bayonet, and scabbard. They were immediately ordered to memorize the serial number. Through repetition, they learned the nomenclature and how to quickly disassemble and reassemble the rifle. Once Marines had learned the basics of their M14s and marksmanship, they began live firing – off-hand (standing) at 100m (109yd), off-hand and kneeling at 200m (219yd), kneeling and sitting at 300m (328yd), and prone at 500m (547yd). At the end of M14 training, they shot for qualification, with 250 points possible; it took 220 points to qualify as Expert, 210 points to qualify as Sharpshooter, and 190 points to qualify as Marksman. According to Emerson, US Marines at the Marine Corps Base, Camp Pendleton, California, and at other bases continued to qualify with the M14 rifle until 1974, and it was still issued to Marines at the 32nd Street Naval Station as late as 1978 (Emerson 2007: 76–77).

Close-up of the M14's rear sight. Troops were trained to set the battle rear sight of the M14 at 250m (273yd) and to use this setting for engagements out to 350m (383yd). This setting would put center of impact 3in high at 100m (109yd), which should still put down an enemy soldier with center of mass aim. Troops were taught at 200m (219yd) to aim for the belt buckle, which put the bullet into the torso. At 250m the sights were "on," while at 300m (328yd) the aiming point was the neck and at 350m the head. These aiming points would give a torso hit. For longer ranges, it was necessary to adjust the elevation dial of the sights. (Author)

THE M14 IN COMBAT

The M14 first saw action in Vietnam as early as 1961, when it was in use with US Army advisors to the South Vietnamese armed forces. It was during this early field use that some of the accuracy, reliability, and parts-breakage problems that would help seal the M14's fate first arose. Use in Vietnam also highlighted the M14's weight and that of its combat load of ammunition, neither of which compared favorably with the AR-15/M16, which was lighter and allowed a combat load of more cartridges. These factors, combined with the heat and humidity and rarity of long-range engagements in Vietnam, made the AR-15/M16 seem very appealing.

Shooting the M14

The safety was applied by pushing it back into the trigger guard (**1**). It was best to get in the habit of doing it with the trigger finger as this allowed the shooter to keep his support hand on the rifle's forearm, permitting faster follow-up shots. Note that unlike many battle rifles, which have a combined fire selector and safety, the M14 had a completely separate selector switch, which allowed the rifle to be set on full-automatic or semiautomatic as desired. When ready to fire the rifle a quick thrust of the finger brought the gun

into action. Normally, troops were trained in combat to have a round chambered and the safety applied, though sentries in locations behind the front line would often have the chamber of their M14 empty and the safety off. In case of an alert they would quickly chamber a round and bring the rifle into action.

Unlike the later M16 and some other rifles, the M14 magazine had to be "rocked" into the magazine well (**2**). This entailed first inserting it at an angle. This system for inserting the magazine is a little slower than magazine wells, such as that on the M16, which allow the magazine to be thrust directly into the weapon; however, with practice the movement became natural. It also allowed the magazine to be inserted with slightly less ground clearance when firing prone. Troops using the rifle were taught that the magazine had to be inserted with forward edge up until the operating-spring guide engaged the magazine before it could be rocked backwards into the locked position. After loading a magazine into the rifle hundreds of times, troops developed the muscle memory to thrust the magazine in at the proper angle and rock it into the locked position smoothly.

The magazine was then pulled towards to the rear to lock it in place (**3**). A distinctive click let the shooter know it was in place. To release the magazine, the magazine-release lever just behind it was pushed forward and the magazine was "rocked" out of the magazine well. Troops used different methods to operate the magazine release, but the simplest and fastest was to grasp the empty magazine and pull it forward and out with the support hand (the left for a right-handed shooter) while pushing the magazine release forward with the thumb of that hand.

With the magazine in place the cocking handle was pulled to the rear, then released to chamber a round (**4**). It was important that the cocking handle was pulled all the way to the rear so it cleared the loaded magazines and that it was released and not ridden forward with the hand, which could cause a failure to chamber the round fully. Various methods could be used to operate the cocking handle. Normally, troops were trained to cock the handle by grasping the forearm with their support hand and pushing the stock tight against the shoulder, after which they would pull the handle back with the shooting hand. In combat, though, some troops learned to reach over or under the rifle with the support hand to operate the cocking handle. Especially in cold weather or if the rifle had been fired a lot, it was a good idea to give the cocking handle a push with the palm to make sure it was fully closed and the rifle was ready to fire (**5**). Many troops gave the cocking handle the extra push every time they loaded a round. In regards to cold weather it should be noted that, as with the M1 Garand, a winter trigger was available for the M14.

The trigger finger pushed the safety forward after it entered the trigger guard; the rifle was aimed, then fired (**6**). Use of the finger was the most natural and fastest method of releasing the safety once it had been practiced, as the operation could be carried out as the trigger entered the trigger guard and before applying pressure to the trigger. Note that there was enough room to slip the finger in between the trigger and safety lever; normally, though, the finger should have been kept out of the trigger guard until ready to fire the weapon. Troops in combat were trained to keep the safety on until ready to fire the weapon, though there was a tendency to flick it off when on patrol to allow faster engagement if ambushed. Whether the safety was on or off when moving with other troops, muzzle awareness was always stressed, yet troops were still injured or killed through negligent discharges of the weapon.

M14s were seeing service, though. Frank Iannamico notes that in July 1963, 175,822 M14 rifles had seen enough use that they needed to be arsenal-rebuilt. Springfield Armory agreed to carry out the rebuilds at $41.00 each based upon the cost of parts and labor. However, since spare parts were not available, the rebuilds required cannibalization of some parts and repair of others. This lowered the cost for the overhaul to $21.71 per rifle. All was not well with the rebuilds, however, as around 30 percent of the rifles failed accuracy requirements. The problems were attributed to various factors, including bent barrels, oversized gas cylinders, undersized gas pistons, and loose clamping of the stock. Springfield Armory corrected the problems and instituted more rigorous quality-control procedures. With experience, the Armory workers became more efficient and reduced direct labor time required to overhaul an M14 to 1.5 hours (Iannamico 2005: 106–07). Springfield Armory received another contract in 1965 to overhaul 24,000 M14 rifles, with H&R receiving a separate contract to target the rifles after Springfield Armory completed the overhaul. Springfield Armory also received an order for spare parts consisting of 64,000 bolts, 35,000 operating rods, and 12,000 stocks, a good indication of parts needing replacement during the overhauls (Iannamico 2005: 107).

During Operation *Taro Leaf* (February 3–15, 1966), US troops, probably of the 25th Infantry Division, call in an airstrike. Both men are armed with M14 rifles. (NARA)

M14s were used by the 1st Infantry Division during combat operations at Lai Khê on November 19, 1965, in Binh Duong Province (Emerson 2007: 70–71). The M14 would continue to be used by US units until at least 1968 in Vietnam; some US Army personnel were armed with the M14 during the Tet Offensive of January 1968. During 1968 and 1969, M14 rifles in the Army seem to have been used primarily by artillery, signals, and aviation units (Emerson 2007: 72). Based on comments by a friend of the author's who was a combat photographer with the 1st Aviation Brigade, they were glad to have the M14s should their helicopters go down in territory controlled by the Viet Cong (VC). Emerson sites the figure of 14,470 M14 rifles and three M14A1 rifles being lost in the Republic of Vietnam between July 1, 1967, and June 30, 1970. These figures include loss for an array of reasons but are indicative that a substantial number of M14s were still in service (Emerson 2007: 73).

An interesting point that arises about the views of troops issued the M14 is preference for the rifles produced by TRW. The author has two friends who were issued the M14 while in the Army, both of whom made it a point to get one made by TRW. Both were shooters who appreciated the difference in performance. Lee Emerson refers to this as the "TRW mystique" and verifies that, generally, TRW-produced M14 rifles were of a higher standard. Among the statistics he cites to make his point are:

– As of August, 1961, M14 failure rates at Springfield Armory, Winchester, and Harrington & Richardson were running between 5 and 12%, while between August, 1962, when TRW began assembling M14 rifles and November, 1962, TRW had no rejections.
– Additionally, in factory test firing, the average five-shot group size for TRW rifles on November, 1962, was 2.5 to 3 inches. (Emerson 2007: 58)

Emerson also points out that TRW had experience in advanced manufacturing techniques, which they applied to the M14, resulting in very few problems during production. Finally, it was TRW that was chosen to produce National Match rifles, an obvious salute to the quality of the rifles produced.

The M14 was fired in anger during the US occupation of the Dominican Republic from April 1965 to July 1966. US Marines were deployed armed

The M1 Garand bayonet was not retained for the M14 rifle; instead, a new bayonet, the M6, was developed. It was, however, similar in design to the M1 Garand's M5 bayonet that had been developed in 1953. Here, two sergeants of Company B-4 of the US Army's 2nd Brigade demonstrate the "On Guard" position with M14 rifles mounting M6 bayonets at Fort Gordon, Georgia, in April 1966. Along with the M4 bayonet for the M1 carbine – which was based on the M3 trench knife – as well as the M5 and later M7 bayonets, the M6 was designed for use as a combat/utility knife as well as a bayonet. Manufacturers for the M6 bayonet included Aerial Cutlery Company, Columbus Milpar and Manufacturing Company, and Imperial Knife Company. The M6 was carried in the M8A1 fiberglass scabbard with a webbed frog; manufacturers included Victory Plastics Company, Viz Manufacturing, and TWB. (NARA)

with the M14, while Army troops of the 82nd Airborne Division had already been armed with the M16. In fighting against revolutionaries of the Dominican Revolutionary Party, US troops suffered 44 killed and over 280 wounded. One of the first engagements occurred shortly after the Marines were heli-lifted into Santo Domingo where they killed two snipers threatening the US Embassy.

During 1965 and 1966, the M14 also saw a great deal of combat with the USMC in Vietnam. One Marine Congressional Medal of Honor winner's view of the M14 in Vietnam was reported in a *Leatherneck* magazine article of December 12, 2005. Captain Robert Modrejewski, who commanded Kilo Company, 3rd Battalion, 4th Marines, won his Medal of Honor during July 15–18, 1966, when his company faced attacks from numerically superior forces of up to regimental strength over a three-day period. Though wounded, Modrejewski crawled through enemy fire to his Marines. Twice, Modrejewski called in "Danger Close" artillery and air support. One factor to which he attributed his troops' survival was the M14, about which he stated: "It was a rifle that you

A left-side view of the M6 bayonet mounted on the M14. The M6 is 11.0375in in overall length and has a 6.0625in blade. Two black polymer grip halves were affixed to the steel bayonet with two machine screws. It had grey Parkerizing – an electrochemical phosphate conversion coating – to protect against corrosion and wear. Once attached by sliding the loop of the bayonet over the M14's flash suppressor, the fit was relatively loose by design so as not to affect accuracy when affixed. Unlike many bayonets that have their release button at the hilt, the M6 uses a lever just behind the crossguard, which allows easier attachment and detachment, as a squeeze with the hand is easier than attempting to press on a release button with the thumb. Also, the hand is in a natural position gripping the handle when attaching or detaching the M6 bayonet. (Author)

US Marines in small boats approach the beach for an amphibious assault in the Rung Sat Zone, 35 miles from Saigon. They are among 1,200 Marines taking part in Operation *Jackstay* during March 1966. (NARA)

could drop in the mud, drop in the dirt. You could drop the magazine, the bullets would get dirty, and yet the weapon would still fire" (Jones 2005).

The Marines appreciated the fact that the M14 was issued with a bayonet, as they retained the traditional Marine willingness to settle matters with cold steel. On January 26, 1967 during Operation *Tuscaloosa*, US Marines encountered the VC B-120 Main Force Battalion. John Culbertson relates one incident during the advance against the VC positions:

> Captain Doherty ordered Gunnery Sergeant Gutierrez to give the command to form the company on line. "ON LINE! THE CAPTAIN WANTS EVERY MARINE ON LINE. FIX BAYONETS. FIRE FROM THE HIP. FORWARD, MARCH. COMMENCE FIRING". Gunny Gutierrez led the Second Platoon in an assault line with Marines abreast firing from the hip as they crossed the final two hundred meters of sand to the second stream. The entire rifle company had joined in

Operation *Wilcox*, August 1966 (previous pages)

These US Marines of the 1st Battalion, 9th Marines fighting in Quảng Nam Province have been taking fire from Viet Cong mortars and are pinned down, but their radioman has called in an airstrike. In the background a USMC Phantom F-4B has just completed a napalm run on Viet Cong positions. The Marine firing from the prone position is firing the M14A1, which was designed to function as a SAW. Because of the large number of casualties suffered by the 9th Marines during the Vietnam War, the highest in USMC history, they were given the nickname "The Walking Dead."

the assault, with Hotel Company picking up some of Foxtrot's stragglers on the way. Nearly two hundred Marines advanced confidently into the second stream.

... As the Marines' assault line entered the stream and came into clear view, the Viet Cong suicide squad opened up from point blank range, sending a short, but deadly, volley into the exposed Marine ranks. One Marine was killed and four others wounded. The enraged Marine riflemen raked the enemy positions with deadly fire, as they scrambled up the clay bank and into the VC trenches. The enemy soldiers who survived the return fire were bayoneted. (Culbertson 2006)

Culbertson made good use of his M14's heavier 7.62×51mm rounds to attack a VC bunker:

PFC Lafley and I crawled up a trail and came under fire from a reinforced bunker to our front. I took the position under fire with my M-14, shooting the parapet to pieces. Moving up, I punched a hole through the bunker and peered in only to see a VC looking back at me. I stepped back and shot him through the chin breaking his neck. An M-79 man fired two rounds into the bunker killing the second VC. PFC John Lafley opened up on a third sniper, and with accurate rifle fire shot a dozen holes in the VC. (Culbertson 2006)

Although the switch to M16 rifles began for the USMC in Vietnam during 1967, some USMC infantry units were still equipped with the M14 into 1968. During the fighting for the city of Huế during February 1968, many of the Marines involved were still using the M14. As with the Army, USMC aviation units retained the M14 longer than most infantry units (Emerson 2007: 77). Another comment on the use of the M14 in the battle of Khe Sanh, January 21–July 9, 1968, by Robert Pisor illustrates the Marines' appreciation for the M14's range and stopping power:

During the Tet Offensive, January 1968, US Marines and Vietnamese forces defend Hamo village. An M14 is visible in the foreground. (NARA)

The men of India Company did not worry about the controversial M-16 because none carried it. Upon arrival at Khe Sanh, they had

traded their M-16s for M-14s, heavier, longer rifles that were being phased out but could still be found in support units. The M-14 could reach five hundred meters from ridgeline to ridgeline with power, while the M-16 – deadly at close range – couldn't seem to find people beyond three hundred meters. (Pisor 1982: 21)

A couple of other points about the M14 in use with the Marines may be noted. On patrols, point men in USMC units often carried select-fire M14s so they could heavily engage when encountering the enemy (Emerson 2007: 75); some, though, still preferred the World War II jungle favorite, the Winchester Model 12 Trench Gun. One friend of the author's who was in the USMC during the Cuban Missile Crisis once told the author that he had managed to "acquire" the parts to make his semiautomatic M14 into a select-fire version, with plans to alter his weapon if he went to war. Another friend who was in the USMC during the Vietnam War continued to carry the M14 as a SAW after the M16 became standard issue.

During 1970 in Vietnam, a Long Range Reconnaissance Patrol (LRRP) team member uses his 'scoped M14 to scan the area around his position. (NARA)

SNIPING VARIANTS AT WAR

Early in the Vietnam War the principal sniping rifle in use with the US Army was the M1D Garand, with some M1903A4 Springfields still in use as well. In 1966, in response to an Army requirement for a replacement, work began on a sniping rifle based on the M14. Initially, some M14 rifles had the M84 telescope used on the Garand, employing the threaded hole and grooves on the left side of the M14's receiver as a mounting point. Ironically, since the M14 had been criticized for lack of accuracy, the replacement for the M1D would be the XM21, later M21, sniping version of the M14. Accuracy was actually relatively good with the M21, as it was based on the M14 National Match rifle.

The XM21/M21

Based on specifications set by the Army Marksmanship Training Unit (AMTU), in about 1966 Rock Island Arsenal converted 1,435 National Match rifles into XM21s by adding a Leatherwood 3–9× ART (adjustable ranging telescope) and supplying National Match ammunition to use with the rifle (Iannamico 2005: 157). Blake Stevens quotes from a document prepared by Colonel Frank Conway of the AMTU relating to the development of the M21:

Approximately two months ago we were contacted by Sgt. Willard of the Limited Warfare Laboratory to see if we would accurize ten M14 rifles that were to be equipped with the "Leatherwood" scope for test in Vietnam. On first contact, we were told that standard issue M14s would be used. Sgt. Willard, who is an old competitive shooter and coach, talked his superiors into using National Match rifles. He personally carried these rifles to Fort Benning and we "worked" them over, just as we do the NM rifles used by the Army Team.

These match-conditioned rifles for the Army Concept Team in Vietnam were then tested by the Test Section in our machine rest (cradle) and averaged 5.3" vertical by 4.7" horizontal at 300 meters with the assigned match ammunition.

The scopes were mounted and zeroed with all rifles checked to about 700 meters. Due to time limitations and range availability shooting was not done beyond this range.

The "self-ranging" Leatherwood scope mounted system works beautifully, with our people being quite enthused over its performance. (Stevens 1995: 281–83)

Iannamico states that a seven-round magazine was issued with the XM21 to allow the sniper to take a lower prone position; however, most photographs of the XM21/M21 show a 20-round magazine in use (Iannamico 2005: 159). To counter the effects of humidity, which would cause the M21's wooden stock to expand and contract and therefore adversely affect accuracy, stocks of the M21 Sniper System used in Vietnam were pressure-impregnated with epoxy, thus making them less sensitive to moisture (Stevens 1995: 270). At least some XM21 rifles used in Vietnam were fitted with SIONICS suppressors. SIONICS stands for Studies In the Operational Negation of Insurgents and Counter-Subversion and applies to suppressors developed by former OSS agent Mitchell WerBell for US Special Forces and other troops including the 9th Infantry Division. They were used to eliminate enemy personnel quietly.

A right-side view of the ART mounted on an M14 rifle. Developed by Lieutenant, later Captain, James Leatherwood when he was assigned to Fort Benning, the ART was designed for use with the Match-grade M14 and the M118 Match cartridge. It was based on a Redfield 3–9× variable-power Accu-Range telescopic sight, with an external cam attached to the power-adjusting ring that sets the 'scope at the correct elevation angle for the M118 Match round at any distance between 300yd (274m) and 900yd (823m). A different reticle was installed (Stevens 1995: 277–78). (John Miller)

A left-side view of the ART used on the XM21, along with the 'scope cover and the 7.62mm Match ammunition intended to be used with the rifle. (John Miller)

March 1967: Serving in I Corps near the Demilitarized Zone bordering North Vietnam, a US Marine sergeant in charge of the sniper team for the 1st Battalion, 9th Marines takes a break during Operation *Prairie II*. Although the Marines began using the XM40 bolt-action sniping rifle in 1966, this sergeant carries a 'scoped M14 rifle, probably built in a USMC armory. (NARA)

The M21 was first issued in 1969 but retained the "XM" experimental designation until officially adopted as the M21 in 1972. It outlasted the M14 by two decades, remaining the primary US Army sniping rifle until 1988 and seeing some use after that. However, the M21 was never really considered a long-range sniping rifle, as normally it was considered most effective at 600m (656yd) or less.

The XM21/M21 sniping rifle was used in Vietnam after the M14 had been replaced with most units. In his excellent *History of Sniping and Sharpshooting*, John Plaster discusses the pros and cons of the XM21:

The ART scope was fairly accurate and fast, but it was also imperfect. Its greatest shortcoming was that its automatic range compensation was synched to a certain magnification. That is, when a shooter employed maximum 9X magnification, he was dead-on only at 900 yards; if he wanted to use 9X at 600 yards, the elliptical cam now put his shot much too high. True, he could disconnect the cam, but then he'd have an ordinary scope and have to compensate by imprecisely holding over his target.

Less critical, the scope's eye relief – the distance between the shooter's eye and the ocular (rear) lens – could not be adjusted because the scope had to be fitted exactly into its cam and mount to work. Thus, a sniper might have to adopt a somewhat unnatural cheekweld for proper eye relief. Another issue, one I often encountered with XM-21 armed sniper students, was difficulty zeroing

the rifle. Since the mount and the scope both had elevation and windage adjustments, students frequently ran out of adjustments in one or the other before they achieved zero. Then an instructor would have to re-center both the mount and the scope to restart the tedious zeroing process.

Still, when fired with the M118 Special Ball Ammunition, the XM-21 shot well and put down many an enemy soldier. My recollection is that our XM-21s fired about 2 inches at 100 yards (2 minutes of angle), and sometimes a bit better, which in that era was excellent for a semiautomatic rifle. (Plaster 2008: 567)

One of the most successful US snipers in Vietnam, Staff Sergeant Adelbert Waldron of the 9th Infantry Division, was credited with 109 enemy kills, the most of any US sniper in the war. Waldron used an XM21 sniping rifle and was especially effective at night in the Mekong Delta where the 9th Infantry Division was assigned. Using an XM21 with an AN/PVS-2 night-vision optic and a SIONICS suppressor, Waldron would choose shooting positions that allowed him to engage the enemy over long distances across the rice paddies (Plaster 2008: 570). US infantry divisions that ran their own sniper schools, such as the 9th and 23rd Infantry divisions, normally issued each graduate with an XM21 sniping rifle (Plaster 2008: 571).

USMC and US Army personnel make final sight adjustments prior to qualifying with their M14 rifles during July 1968, at the 3rd Marine Division Sniper School at Quảng Tri, South Vietnam. Once they have proven their marksmanship with iron sights they can move on to the 'scoped sniping rifle. (NARA)

An official photograph of the XM21 with 'scope and 'scope cover. The 'scope mount for the XM21 would accommodate the ART day 'scope or the AN/PVS-2 night 'scope, thus allowing a sniper to use either depending on whether he would be operating during the day or at night. (NARA)

During April 1968, a soldier of the 31st Infantry Division focuses his Starlight Scope on an object of known distance prior to beginning night guard duty along the Demilitarized Zone in Korea. (NARA)

Although USMC snipers in Vietnam primarily used Winchester Model 70 or Remington Model 700 sniping rifles, Emerson points out that there were instances when the M14 gave scout-sniper teams urgently needed firepower:

> Nonetheless, the M14 rifle was no strange bedfellow to Marine Corps scout-snipers in the Republic of Viet Nam. 4th Marine Regiment scout-sniper teams of two to five carried and used select fire capable M14 rifles along with the issue bolt action sniper rifles during operations from November 1966 until at least January 1968 in Quang Tri and Thua Thien Provinces. Likewise, 5th Marine Regiment scout-sniper team observers put the M14 rifle to good use against the Viet Cong R20 Main Force Battalion in the Song Thu Bon valley of Quang Tri province while in support of Marine rifle companies during Operation Tuscaloosa in late January and early February 1967. The M14 rifles provided the necessary firepower to break contact with the enemy at close range. (Emerson 2007: 118)

In summing up the effectiveness of the XM21/M21 sniping rifle in Vietnam, Blake Stevens quotes from a July 26, 1971, issue of *U.S. News and World Report*: "An average expenditure of 1.34 rounds per kill by 9th Division Snipers was reported (with the M21), as compared to an average

Operation *Just Cause*, December 1989 (opposite)

Here, an enemy sniper has fired on US troops in Panama City. As a result, a US NCO with sniper training has grabbed an M21 sniping rifle. Paired with another soldier to act as a spotter, he has taken up a position in a room on one of the upper floors of a high-rise building to engage the sniper. The US sniper has only his pistol belt and Beretta M9, while the observer is armed with an M16 rifle. The sniper is using a pillow from a couch as an improvised rest and is firing from a kneeling position.

expenditure of 31,900 pounds of ammunition per enemy casualty in Vietnam. There are eighteen 7.62 mm, or forty 5.56 mm, rounds in one pound" (Stevens 1995: 313).

Joe Poyer points out a typical example of how military record-keeping caused the XM21 rifle to be considered too fragile for combat. Standard practice was to engrave the rifle's serial number on the 'scope and mount. This was done not because the rifle had to be used with that specific 'scope and mount, but as a record-keeping aid, though the fact that the 'scope and mount were mated for zeroing as discussed above may have instilled the belief they could not be separated. However, in Vietnam, if a problem occurred with the 'scope or the mount, as no spare parts were available, armorers – not wanting to remove the numbered sight and mount from the rifle, even if they had spare 'scopes or mounts – declared the entire rifle unserviceable. This problem was solved in 1970 when the AMTU put out a bulletin informing armorers and others in the chain of command that there was no reason for not replacing a damaged 'scope or mount with another one if available (Poyer 2000: 18).

John Plaster also relates the use of an M21 sniping rifle during Operation *Just Cause* when US forces went into Panama in 1989–90. A Panamanian sniper in a high-rise building had taken US troops under fire when Sergeant First Class John Lucas of the 82nd Airborne Division, a sniper in Vietnam with 38 confirmed kills, took an M21 and ascended to the 15th floor of the Marriott Hotel building, from where he spotted the sniper at about 750m (820yd) and killed him with one shot (Plaster 2008: 601–02). US Army Rangers also used the M21 during October 1983, when they parachuted into Grenada.

Perhaps the best-known use of an M14 sniping rifle in combat occurred during the battle of Mogadishu, Somalia, in October 3–4, 1993. A force of US Army Rangers supported by other US Special Operations Forces, including operators of 1st Special Forces Operational Detachment Delta, attempted to seize two of Mohamed Farrah Aidid's lieutenants. During the assault, two UH-60 Black Hawk helicopters were downed by Somali militiamen. An attempt to rescue the downed crewmen turned into a battle that would last overnight and result in 18 US killed, 80 wounded, and one helicopter pilot captured. Estimates of Somali casualties have run as high as 3,000, though the Somalis only admitted to around 1,100.

At the second crash site, two Delta snipers, Master Sergeant Gary Gordon and Sergeant First Class Randy Shughart, were giving overwatch sniper cover; however, when it became apparent that a Somali mob would reach the helicopter and likely kill any survivors, the two snipers were inserted to give covering fire for the survivors until help could arrive. After removing the injured crewmen from the helicopter, the two snipers began to engage the Somalis. Using their accurized M14 rifles, the two snipers held off the Somalis until they ran out of ammunition and were overrun and killed. Accounts say that the two snipers were using accurized M14s, rather than M21s; these may have been rifles built by Delta armorers, possibly the XM25 Sniper Weapon System developed in 1991 for the Special Forces and SEALs. Both men posthumously received the Congressional Medal of Honor for their sacrifice.

The M25

Another sniping version of the M14 was developed in about 1991 for use by the US Army Special Forces, though it was also used by the US Navy SEALs. Each XM25 rifle was built as virtually a custom rifle; each service added its own touches. These rifles were based on M14s built to National Match specifications and had the barreled actions glass-bedded into a McMillan fiberglass stock, creating a more stable fit for better accuracy. Other improvements included a National Match spring guide and a Brookfield Precision Tools 'scope mount, and premium barrels from manufacturers such as Douglas, Hart, and Krieger were used. The standard 'scope was a Leupold Ultra Mk 4 or Vari-X III LR. An OPS, Inc. suppressor was sometimes used on the M25. Estimates are that around 200 were built (Johnston & Nelson 2010: 989). Trigger pulls were tuned to 4.5lb Match specifications. The M25 has continued in use with US Special Operations Forces until the present. As with the M21, however, the M25 has been mostly superseded for longer-range use by other sniping rifles. Though production of the M14 had ceased, some development would continue in recent years as M14s were pulled from armories and upgraded as DMRs.

THE M14 SINCE 9/11

During the "War on Terror," the M14 has gained new life; however, the number of rifles remaining in US armories is surprisingly small considering that 1,380,346 were produced (Johnston & Nelson 2010: 976). As M14 rifles were replaced by the M16, many were destroyed, reportedly 750,000 between 1970 and the present day, while another 450,000 had been supplied to foreign military forces by 1999 (see below). Of those remaining in US military hands, the USAF retains around 3,500 for use by drill

Firing a 'scoped M14 aboard USS *Mahan* in May 2007; *Mahan* is a destroyer, so it is possible that this M14 is kept aboard for exploding mines as well as for use in various security situations. (US Navy)

teams, USAF Pararescue, Combat Control Teams, and EOD personnel for destroying explosives at longer range. US Navy ships normally have a couple of M14s each for line-throwing or exploding mines at a distance and more recently for anti-piracy duties; the USMC retains at least 3,000. As of 2007, the US Army had 22,660 M14s in service, while another 87,462 remained in storage. Some drill teams use the M14 as do Opposing Forces (OPFOR) aggressor units, cadets at the US Military Academy, and the 1st Battalion/3rd US Infantry Regiment, which does ceremonial guard duties at Arlington National Cemetery (Eger 2009). M14s are also used as Army DMRs. The largest group of M14s still in use, though, is made up of those functioning as DMRs.

During the 1990s, the USMC first saw the advantage of choosing Marines who were excellent marksmen and arming them with a rifle capable of better accuracy than the M16. Though not trained in stalking and camouflage to the extent of a true sniper, the designated marksman does give the infantry squad the capability of effectively engaging the enemy at longer distances. According to the US Army's Sergeant First Class Jeremy Mangione, "The SDM is expected to accomplish many of the same shooting tasks as a sniper, with out the help of a more experienced spotter. The work of two experienced soldiers, in effect, needs to be done with one minimally experienced soldier" (Mangione 2010). The need for the DMR in Afghanistan was described succinctly by Staff Sergeant John Hawes of C Troop, 3-71 RSTA (Reconnaissance, Surveillance, and Target Acquisition), 10th Mountain Division on the website Pro Patria:

> I agree that there is a marksmanship gap at the unit level from 300–600m [328–656yd] as mentioned and believe the Designated Marksman at squad level is a possible answer to this. In Afghanistan, we had multiple engagements (I would say vast majority of our engagements) with the enemy (were) from beyond 300m. A-lot of engagements took place on our re-supply convoys/vehicle patrols. The enemy in these cases always had the high ground because all roads in my AO were in river valleys and followed the river on the valley floor. The terrain was too steep to possibly make a road on higher ground. With the enemies high ground advantage it was like they were shooting fish in a barrel. They only had to spend a quick second exposing themselves to dump a magazine of AK ammo down in our general direction before dropping behind cover or the crest of the ridge or hill they were on and out of our sight and then they would just repeat until we brought in-direct fires on them. Rifle fire/crew served weapons was of little effect on them in most cases. I attribute this to three reasons. Lack of marksmanship ability past 300m for which our standard weapons are zeroed at, lack of knowledge on how to engage or lead a moving or pop-up target, and angle firing. (Quoted in Anon 2013b)

A 2009 US Army report asserted that 50 percent of Army engagements in Afghanistan occur with the enemy attacking at 300m (328yd) or beyond, while more than 80 percent of soldiers in an infantry company are equipped with weapons that can't touch the enemy beyond that range:

These operations occur in rugged terrain and in situations where traditional supporting fires are limited due to range or risk of collateral damage. With these limitations, the infantry in Afghanistan require a precise, lethal fire capability that exists only in a properly trained and equipped infantryman. The thesis of this paper is that while the infantryman is ideally suited for combat in Afghanistan, his current weapons, doctrine and marksmanship training do not provide a precise, lethal fire capability to 500 meters and are therefore inappropriate. (Earhart 2009: 1)

Iraq, November 2007: A designated marksman of the 22nd Infantry Regiment; both rifle and 'scope are camouflaged. (USAF)

Earhart goes on to say:

Operations in Afghanistan have exposed weaknesses in our small arms capability, marksmanship, and doctrine. After-action reviews and comments from returning non-commissioned officers and officers reveal that about fifty per cent of engagements occur past 300 meters. The enemy tactics are to engage U.S. forces from high ground with medium and heavy weapons, often including mortars, knowing that we are restricted by our equipment limitations and the inability of our overburdened soldiers to maneuver at elevations exceeding 6,000 feet. Current equipment, training, and doctrine are optimized for engagements under 300 meters on a level terrain. (Earhart 2009: 24)

Currently, the M14 continues to fill a niche within the US Armed Forces for a special-purpose rifle granting longer-range and greater striking power than the M4/M16. Although Afghanistan provided impetus for development of the various DMR- and EBR- (enhanced battle rifle) type rifles, it is likely that at least some M14 variations will remain in use once US troops have left Afghanistan. The US Army's Squad Designated Marksmanship Course, a ten-day training program, is held at Fort Benning, Georgia:

The focus of the course is on the soldier's need to engage targets rapidly at 300–600m with accurate fires under day and night conditions. The program begins with the fundamentals of marksmanship and progresses to more rapid and accurate engagements employing the individual rifle ... This is conducted at Ft. Benning, Georgia on our 600 meter Known Distance Range and local machine gun ranges. This allows the Warfighter to focus on the fundamentals of shooting while receiving feedback for shots fired and culminates with the practical application of all the principles taught in an environment with unknown distance, limited exposure and only natural environmental feedback indicators. (USAMU no date)

The USMC DMR

The basis of the USMC DMR was the M14 built to Match specifications by the USMC Precision Weapons Shop at Quantico, Virginia. Bedded in a McMillan Tactical M2A fiberglass stock with pistol grip and adjustable cheek piece, the DMR is equipped with a Harris bipod, a Unertl M40 or Leupold & Stevens Mk 4 10× 'scope mounted on a special MIL-STD-1913 Picatinny rail, a 22in Krieger Match-grade barrel, and a Harris bipod. The USMC DMR can also mount the AN/PVS-10 or AN/PVS-17 night vision 'scope. Designated marksmen were issued M118LR ammunition. The DMR has also been used by members of USMC scout-sniper teams on missions where the ability to deliver multiple rounds quickly is desirable, or by the spotter on a sniper team.

The M39 EMR

In 2008, the DMR in use with the USMC was replaced by the M39 EMR. Basically, the M39 EMR is the same rifle as the DMR but with an upgraded metal stock that allows adjustment for length and height to enable establishment of a better cheek weld for the marksman. The standard optical sight is the M8541 scout-sniper day 'scope (Schmidt &

Bender 3–12×50mm PM II) used with the USMC M40A3 bolt-action sniping rifle. Also, a heavier-duty version of the Harris bipod is used on the EMR. The USMC has also used the SAM-R (squad advanced marksman rifle), which is a more accurate version of the M16. Generally, the SAM-R was used in Iraq and the DMR or EMR was employed in Afghanistan, where the engagement ranges tended to be longer.

The Mk 14 Mod 0 EBR

A special version of the M14 developed for US Navy and USMC special warfare personnel is designated the Mk 14 Mod 0 EBR. These rifles were rebuilt to specifications developed at the Small Arms Weapons Branch, Ordnance Engineering Directorate at the Navy's Surface Warfare Center, Crane, Indiana. M14 rifles were first selected, disassembled, and inspected. Some standard parts were retained and others were not. Using the basic M14 action, Mk 14 Mod 0 EBRs use an 18in barrel, made by Springfield Armory of Geneseo, Illinois, instead of the standard 22in barrel. A Sage International Chassis Stock System with pistol grip replaces the wooden stock. Since the rifle was designed for use by US Navy and USMC special operators, for greater corrosion resistance, original parts that are reused are coated with manganese phosphate and the gas cylinder was coated with black oxide. Wolff springs replace the GI springs, trigger parts were polished, and trigger pull adjusted to 4.5–7.5lb. Other replacement parts include a Sage International operating-rod guide, a Smith Enterprise, Incorporated (SEI) flash suppressor, and a new rear-sight aperture from XS Sight Systems. Additional enhancements include a military-standard 1913 Picatinny rail, improved iron sights, see-through 'scope rings, Harris bipod, and tactical sling (Iannamico 2005: 117–19).

US Marines in Afghanistan, during April 2011, fire the USMC M39 EMR. The stock is adjustable for length and height for the optimal cheek weld. The 'scope is the USMC M8541 Scout Sniper Day Scope (SSDS) (Schmidt & Bender 3–12×50mm), which was originally designed for use on the bolt-action M40A3 sniping rifle, and the bipod is the heavy-duty version of the Harris S-L. (US DOD)

The Mk 14 Mod 2 EBR-EDMV

The Navy uses other variations of the EBR. For example, the Naval
Expeditionary Combat Command (NECC) had used the M14 SSR (sniper
support rifle). However, a more sophisticated rifle was developed by Naval
Surface Warfare Center Crane Small Arms Engineering Section for NECC,
which is now designated the Coastal Riverine Force (CRG). Designated the
Mk 14 Mod 2 EBR-EDMV (enhanced battle rifle – expeditionary
designated marksman variant), this rifle was designed for a variety of
missions including overwatch for VBSS, perimeter defense, ordnance stand-
off (i.e. exploding devices from a distance), and security of command posts.
This rifle is normally equipped with either the AN/PVS-27 night vision
'scope or the NightForce NXS 3.5–15×50mm day 'scope. Accuracy is 1½
MoA (1.5in group at 100yd – roughly 38mm at 91m) or less.

The USAF acquired a small number of EMRs from the Navy for use
by EOD personnel. USAF EOD also uses the M14 SMUD. However, the
USAF Special Tactics squadrons also have their own version of the EBR
– the Mk 14 Mod 0. The US Coast Guard uses a rifle with some similarities
to the Mk 14, which is designated the M14 Tactical but has a 22in barrel
using the SEI flash suppressor.

Operation *Enduring Freedom*, March 2011 (previous pages)

In Afghanistan's Nangarhar Province, troops of the US 34th Infantry Division (National Guard)
are questioning villagers about a supply stockpile near the village. Soldiers providing
overwatch for those questioning the villagers spot a Taliban sniper armed with an SVD rifle
at about 200yd (183m). The SVD or Dragunov has been used by the Russians and client
states as a sniping rifle for decades, though it is actually more of a DMR than a true sniping
rifle. It is self-loading and chambers the 7.62×54mmR cartridge. Even with the specially
loaded sniping ammunition available for it, it is not equivalent to Western sniper rifles. The
designated marksman in the middle of the overwatch group prepares to eliminate the Taliban
sniper with his EBR. The other two soldiers on overwatch will engage the other Taliban
supporting the sniper using their M4 carbines.

The M14SE

Still another M14 rebuild is the SEI "Crazy Horse" rifle, also known as the M14SE. These are upgraded standard M14 rifles, as SEI states:

> Our strategic intent with this project has been to offer current M-14 users a thoroughly reliable, proven and cost-effective modernization program as a compelling, cost-effective and fast track course of action for a modern 7.62mm NATO caliber Squad Designated Marksman (SDM). Our customers have proven in combat that the M14SE will fulfill this same tactical mission as a new production 7.62mm NATO SDM would be required to accomplish at one-third to one-half the price. (SEI no date)

An M14-armed Colombian Marine, a member of one of many foreign armed forces that received M14s from the USA. (US DOD)

FOREIGN USE OF THE M14

The M14 has seen widespread use outside the USA through aid to friendly governments. South American countries that have used the M14 include Argentina, Colombia, Costa Rica, Dominican Republic, Ecuador, El Salvador, Honduras, and Venezuela. A substantial number of M14 rifles were supplied to Lithuania and have been used by that country's armed forces since it entered NATO. In Africa, Eritrea, Ethiopia, Morocco, Niger, and Tunisia have used the M14. In Asia, US allies South Korea, Taiwan, and the Philippines have employed the M14. According to Johnson & Nelson (2010: 999), Taiwan received 173,729 M14s prior to 1977 as well as producing up to one million Type 57 versions themselves. The Type 57 was produced on the former H&R machinery, which was sold to the State Arsenal of the Republic of China in 1968. The Philippines also received 104,000 M14s prior to 1974 (Johnson & Nelson 2010: 999). During the Vietnam War, M14s were supplied to ARVN (Army of the Republic of Vietnam) forces, but they proved unpopular with the smaller-statured Vietnamese owing to the weapon's size and recoil. Israel and Greece have used the M14, and some US allies have used M14-based sniping rifles or DMRs.

IMPACT
A lasting influence

ASSESSING THE M14'S EFFECTIVENESS

Official responses

It is interesting to note some comments from a December 1962 *Rifle Evaluation Study* by the United States Army Combat Developments Command:

> – The M14 (USAIB) is a definite improvement over the M14 (M) in the automatic rifle role and in the few tests conducted has shown itself superior to the AR-15 in the automatic rifle role at ranges beyond 400 meters.
> – The AK-47 is basically a submachine gun and is inferior to both the M14, M14 (USAIB), and AR-15 in range effectiveness, ammunition lethality and other desired rifle characteristics.
> – The round fired by the M14 family has been adopted as NATO standard small arms ammunition. A sampling test by U.S. Army, Europe showed interchangeability of NATO rounds among various national makes.
> – U.S. Army Forces in Europe are completely equipped with the M14 rifle.
> – At the end of Fiscal Year 1962, the U.S. Army had an inventory of about 415,000 M14 rifles. This will increase to about 735,000 rifles by the end of Fiscal Year 1963. The production base approximates 375,000 a year and the current production objective is about 2,500,000 M14 rifles by the end of Fiscal Year 1969. (US Army 1962a: 5)

Note that the "M14 (USAIB)" (US Army Infantry Board) refers to what would come to be known as the M14A1. Note also that the study mentions projected production of 2,500,000 M14 rifles when only 1,380,346 were actually produced. The study includes a conclusion that the AR-15 should be improved and adopted for air-assault, airborne, and special-forces units, while any units deployed to Europe should be issued the M14 (US Army 1962a: 6). It is also interesting that this study seems to view the AR-15 as the weapon to fulfill the niche intended for the prototype folding-stock versions of the M14.

Critical verdicts

Although some articles in *The American Rifleman* had been relatively laudatory about the M14, other articles were not. An April 1963 article in *True Magazine* was especially critical of the M14 program. The article's lead sentence immediately lets the reader know the author's thesis: "After nearly 20 years of Pentagon bungling that has cost US taxpayers over $100 million so far, the Army is issuing out GIs a new automatic rifle that experts think is inferior to the gun we already have" (Tompkins 1963). Among the "problems" with the M14 cited in the article are the tight tolerances of its gas system – seven times tighter than the M1 Garand. Tompkins states, "On a piece of machinery like a rifle this tightness invites trouble" (Tompkins 1963). However, he never specifies what that "trouble" is. Presumably he means it will lead to malfunctions, but he cites no test results to back this up. Later in the article he cites "expert opinion" that the gas system slowed M14 production.

December 19, 1961: Private First Class Kenneth Long of the 3rd Infantry Division demonstrates the new M14 rifle at Fort Myer, Virginia. (NARA)

Tompkins' final criticism is that despite all of the efforts to develop a select-fire battle rifle, nine out of ten M14s issued were set to fire only on semiautomatic. Most experienced shooters, including the present author, would argue that this was not a bad thing but a good one. It takes a great deal of training to be able to fire accurately on full-automatic, and, even then, it is normally with bursts. Many troops given a select-fire weapon have a tendency to set in on full-automatic and spray down range. This is a waste of ammunition, and loaded M14 magazines were heavy to carry. Those M14s with the selector switch were normally in the hands of troops who had demonstrated some ability to fire on full-automatic. They were used as a SAW, much as the BAR had been in World War II and Korea. Tompkins' point must be granted some validity, however, given that one of the primary arguments for replacing the M1 Garand was to gain select-fire capability for every infantryman. He argues that if the Army

Although the M14 was designed to feed by detachable box magazines, those magazines could be re-charged while in the rifle from stripper clips. (John Miller)

were going to issue a semiautomatic rifle, why not keep the M1 Garand but with a detachable magazine? Tompkins ends with what is admittedly a pithy summation of the issuance of semiautomatic M14s to most troops, referring to the switch that had to be installed before the weapon could offer full-automatic fire: "If you get your hands on a semi-automatic M14 remember that company commanders are supposed to carry extra switches with them in case of an enemy charge. This ought to work out just dandy – especially on dark nights" (Tompkins 1963).

The troops' views

Among both Army and USMC personnel there were many who did not like the replacement of the M14 by the M16. The feeling was that the M16 did not offer the knockdown power of the M14 and that it was less reliable. This was especially true among the first units to receive M16s, as these weapons did not have the chromed chambers to inhibit corrosion and troops were not trained in properly maintaining the M16s.

In January 1967, the US Army issued a Technical Note on *Small Arms Use in Vietnam: M14 Rifle and .45-Caliber Pistol*. Based on surveys of soldiers and Marines who had used the M14 in combat, the comments are quite illuminating about the M14. A selection of comments on what was needed are offered below:

– Fiberglass or other form of stock for M-14, which can withstand the beating an infantry man dishes out.
– A lighter automatic rifle with lightweight magazines made of an alloy which would be more resistant to rust.
– A better mag for the M-14. A plastic mag. would be better.
– A lighter faster firing rifle than the M14.
– The M14 is too big and heavy for jungle warfare.
– What would help me most is a weapon, lighter than the M14 and more compact. It must be as durable and accurate as the M14, and be effective to at least 400 meters, and preferably 500.

Two troops firing the M14 from the prone position; note that the protruding magazine does not let them get as low as they could have gotten with the M1 Garand. (NARA)

– Smaller caliber than the 7.62 NATO but larger than the M16 with more accuracy. The weapon should be made of more rust resistant alloy.
– Everything that I have here meets my needs. No other weapon can compete with the M14.
– The M14 is about the best weapon that an infantryman can use.
– Newer ammunition. Wood on rifle stocks for M14 is swelling too much in rain. After taking rifle apart it is impossible to put it back together without drying the stock first.
– I think we should have a weapon as accurate as the M14 if not more that wouldn't rust as easy as the M14.
– The M-14 does not function properly in rainy weather. Mud seems to clog action. The weapon also seems to rust heavily and slow down rate of fire.
– The M-14 rifle is capable of doing the job. However, because of the climatic condition here, along with the terrain, rust is a major problem. If there is some way of combating this then the combat marine would greatly appreciate the information. (US Army 1967: 8–15)

The selection of comments listed above gives a snapshot of the general feeling of troops using the M14 in Vietnam. Although some liked the M14, in general, troops found that it was heavy and too susceptible to rusting or the wooden stock swelling in the conditions found in Vietnam. Many of the respondents, who were not quoted, expressed a desire to be issued the M16, though some specifically said they preferred the M14 but wanted to see action to address its shortcomings.

THE M14 AND ITS COMPARATORS

In evaluating the M14, it must be viewed in context with the other rifles that can be considered its rivals. These would primarily consist of the FN FAL, the G3, and the AK-47, though the SKS might also be mentioned. It should be borne in mind when discussing the pros and cons of the M14 versus these other rifles that the M14's adoption was not just influenced by military factors but by political factors within the US Department of Defense (DOD) and NATO.

The author firing the HK91, the semi-auto version of the G3, during a demonstration of how fast the Munich terrorists could have been eliminated had the G3 been properly employed. This test was fired for a documentary on the 1972 Olympic tragedy. At Fürstenfeldbruck Air Base in Germany where the terrorists took the hostages to board a plane, and where the final assault by the German police resulted in the death of all hostages, one policeman was in a concealed position about 50yd (46m) from the terrorists as they exited the helicopters. This test was carried out to show that the G3 rifle, with which some of the police were armed, was sufficiently accurate and fast-firing to be used to eliminate the terrorists before they could turn their weapons on the hostages. (Author)

Ergonomics and soldier-friendliness

Based on the author's experience with these rifles, an important factor in favor of the FAL, G3, and AK-47 versus the M14 is the inclusion of a pistol grip. Although the M14A1 version of the M14 did include a pistol-grip stock, most M14s retained the same type of stock as the M1 Garand. As a result, it was much harder to control when being fired in full-auto mode. Additionally, the pistol grip allows the soldier easily to carry the rifle with one hand, yet bring it back into action quickly. The combination of the pistol grip and the balance of the FAL and AK-47 make them handier for quick-reaction shooting and engaging multiple targets more rapidly.

One plus for the M14 is its safety, which protrudes into the trigger guard and may be easily operated with the back of the trigger finger. FAL and G3 safeties are relatively easy to operate with the thumb of the shooting hand but – especially with the G3 – may require some shifting of the shooting grip. The AK-47 safety may be operated with the trigger finger or thumb before assuming the shooting position, but is normally slower than the others.

All three of the NATO battle rifles, as well as the AK-47, have a lever magazine release that may be operated with the trigger finger or the thumb of the support hand. The release on the FAL is smaller than those on the G3, M14, or AK-47, which may make it slightly harder to operate. For overall length and handiness, the AK-47 gets the nod, as the M14, FAL, and G3 are all good-sized rifles. Since to do a thorough cleaning, the M14's action must be removed from the stock, maintenance is more complicated than with the FAL, which may be broken open, or the AK-47, which may have the top cover removed to give access to the recoil spring and bolt. Since the G3 also requires removal of the stock, it shows no advantage over the M14.

Another characteristic that could be considered as an ergonomic issue is the adaptability for use by airborne troops. Although there were attempts to create a version of the M14 for use by paratroopers, they really did not get past the testing stage. On the other hand, a Para version of the FN FAL was developed with a side folding stock; a *Fallschirmjäger* version of the G3 was designed with a collapsible stock; and a *Desantnik* version of the AK-47 was developed with an under-folding stock.

Accuracy, range, and stopping power

Generally, the M14, G3, and FAL are considered more accurate than the AK-47, which may be attributed to various factors, including the sights and ammunition. The HK G3 rear sight is a diopter, which, combined with the hooded post front sight, allows a good sight picture. Also in favor of the G3 are ridges on the top of its receiver, which allow the easy mounting of an optical sight. The M14's adjustable rear sight allows the rifle to be fired quite accurately once zeroed. The FAL's aperture rear sight is more basic and makes precise aiming more difficult. Likewise, the post front and sliding rear-sight notch of the AK-47 do not make for the most precise shooting. Adjustment for windage and elevation with the AK-47 requires moving the front sight.

Normally, the 7.62×51mm NATO ammunition used in the NATO battle rifles is more accurate than 7.62×39mm ammunition used in the AK-47, though standard military ammunition is not known for precision. When Match ammunition is used in an M14, accuracy improves quite a bit, especially if fitted with a telescopic sight. The rifles chambered for the 7.62×51mm NATO round also have greater range and striking power than the AK-47, due to the latter's less powerful cartridge. On the other hand, the standard magazine capacity for the 7.62×51mm rifles is 20 rounds, while the standard for the AK-47 is 30 rounds. There were 30-round magazines available for the FN FAL Squad Automatic Weapon, though; these could also be used in the standard FAL.

The FN FAL is an excellent rifle, though its sights are normally not as good as those of the M14 or G3. Though handy and fast-handling, at 43in in overall length the FAL is a difficult weapon to use in confined spaces or to stow well for airborne, airmobile, or seaborne operations. For this reason the Para version with folding stock was developed. (Courtesy of Rock Island Auction Service)

Inexpensive training and smaller-caliber versions

The ability to train troops less expensively, especially on indoor ranges, makes sub-caliber conversion units an important adjunct to a military rifle. Both the G3 and FAL had sub-caliber conversion units, which could be installed to allow the rifles to fire .22 long-rifle ammunition in training. For the AK-47, some countries actually produced .22 long-rifle versions of the rifle, which used the same sights and operated in the same way as the 7.62×39mm versions. On the other hand, there was not a conversion unit or sub-caliber version of the M14, which limited its use on many indoor ranges and required the use of more expensive 7.62×51mm ammunition for all training.

When the NATO standard cartridge became the 5.56×45mm round instead of the 7.62×51mm, the G3 rifle's basic design could be used to create the HK33 in the smaller caliber. FN did not retain the FAL design but developed the FNC rifle, which used an operating system similar to that of the Kalashnikov. Retaining the basic AK-47 operating system, the AK-74 rifle in 5.45×39mm was developed. Of course, a smaller-caliber version of the M14 was not developed, as the M16 was its 5.56×45mm replacement.

Production considerations

Designed for ease of production and low cost, the AK-47 may be produced in large numbers and because of its simplicity requires less maintenance than other rifles. The FN FAL, on the other hand, requires substantial machining and is more costly. For comparison, about two million FALs have been built, while, reportedly, more than 100 million AK-47s have been produced. As with most German weapons, the G3 shows high-

quality production, which also increases price and requires expertise for manufacture. The M14 was relatively expensive to produce, though there was some carryover in expertise from producing the M1 Garand. Use of a polymer stock on the G3 and many FALs made the rifles less susceptible to problems in humid climates, though the AK-47, which normally had a wood stock, served well in many jungle wars, aided by its looser tolerances. Initially, the M14 used a wooden stock, which had a tendency to swell when used in Southeast Asia. Many currently used M14-based DMRs have polymer stocks.

The author demonstrating the use of the AK-47 bayonet on an unloaded folding-stock version of the rifle. Although the AK-47 is 35in overall with fixed stock, in folding-stock configuration, it is only 25.4in overall. This makes it a concealable weapon and one easily carried when parachuting or fast roping, but the folding stock is not comfortable for shooting and has some tendency to rattle, which can give away the soldier's movements. (Author)

The author's experience

Based on the author's own use of the four rifles under discussion, he has a preference for the FN FAL, especially the Para model with folding stock. Mostly, this is subjective because he finds the FAL feels good in the hands and allows fast, instinctive shooting. He also likes the AK-47 because of its toughness and ability to keep operating under harsh conditions. When in the current DMR format, the M14 with a modern pistol-grip stock is a very effective rifle, and with good optical sights and ammunition can be the most accurate of the four rifles, but it is still heavy and somewhat unwieldy. He has shot the G3 the least of the four, at least partially because he likes it the least. The roller action causes recoil to be more pronounced and also seems to make the rifle move in the hand more, making follow-up shots more difficult. These characteristics are magnified when firing it on full-automatic.

The SKS rifle

The SKS is not really an assault rifle or battle rifle, but instead a late World War II development that was used for decades by the Soviets and various client states. Unlike the other rifles under discussion here, it was a semiautomatic (though for most users so was the M14) and did not have a detachable box magazine but instead had a fixed ten-round magazine that was fed by stripper clips. It was chambered for the 7.62×39mm round that would later be used in the AK-47 and thus remained in service as a second-line weapon after the AK-47 was adopted. As a result of the chambering for the corrosive 7.62×39mm round, SKS barrels are normally chrome-lined. One feature that is quite useful for a rifle widely issued to militias and insurgent groups is that the SKS incorporates an integral folding bayonet, thus precluding the need for issuing a separate bayonet and scabbard.

If one had access to any of the battle rifles discussed above, the SKS would not seem especially desirable, but as a "people's rifle" it offers a

The M14 can be quite accurate in the National Match version. National Match versions of the rifle had selected parts and barrels and were carefully assembled to enhance accuracy. The adjustable rear sight on the National Match version was also more precise. National Match M14s were fitted with optical sights and issued with Match ammunition when issued as the M21. Shown is a National Match version of the Springfield Armory M1A. (Author)

simple, less expensive choice that – like the AK-47 – will continue to function under adverse conditions. It has also proven extremely popular in the USA as a light hunting and self-defense rifle, as many surplus SKSs have been sold there.

TECHNICAL INFLUENCE

Arguably, the greatest influence of the M14 has been in its caliber. The 7.62×51mm NATO round – .308 Winchester in its commercial, sporting loading – has proven one of the most popular military loadings in history, and in the USA and Canada especially has been widely used as a hunting load. Development work on what would become the 7.62×51mm NATO round began not long after World War I as the US began development of a semiautomatic rifle, development that would eventually result in the M1 Garand. Initially, it was felt that the .30-06 service cartridge in use with the M1903 Springfield rifle and the BAR would be difficult to adapt to a self-loading rifle light enough for infantry use. During the first years of development of the self-loading rifle the .276 Pederson round was considered a possible replacement, but eventually the M1 Garand proved reliable with the .30-06 cartridge and it was retained through World War II.

A selection of ammunition available for use in the M14 or XM21 rifle. (John Miller)

The development of a replacement for the Garand would result in the adoption of the M14 rifle. To allow the use of a shorter receiver, a round based on the .30-06 but with a case .5in (13mm) shorter was developed. The basis of the 7.62×51mm round was actually the sporting .300 Savage case, which had been designed for use in lever-action rifles. All three cartridges have the same .470in (12mm) case base diameter.

69

The round developed was designated the T65 and produced ballistics very similar to those of the .30-06 round as the T65 fired a 147-grain (9.52g) bullet at 2,750ft/sec (838m/sec), while the M2 ball round for the .30-06 fired a 151-grain (9.78g) bullet at 2,740ft/sec (835m/sec). Use of more modern propellants allowed the 7.62×51mm to achieve better ballistics in the shorter case. Although the British had developed their own .280 round, and the Belgians and Canadians also wanted a 7mm (.280) round, the United States insisted on the adoption of the 7.62×51mm round as the NATO standard, which it became in 1954. However, the 7.62×51mm round still caused enough recoil and muzzle rise that its use on full-automatic fire for more than short bursts was very problematic. On the positive side, the 7.62×51mm round proved very reliable in full-automatic fire and remains the chambering for NATO medium machine guns such as the FN MAG, US M60 and M240 (the US version of the MAG), and German MG3 among others. Because of the size and weight of loaded 7.62×51mm magazines for the M14, G3, and FAL, which normally held 20 rounds, the infantryman was limited in the number of spare magazines he could carry. The 7.62×51mm has proved to be accurate enough that most modern sniping rifles are chambered in this cartridge, though there has been a trend towards using sniping rifles chambered for the .300 Winchester Magnum and .338 Lapua Magnum to gain longer-range striking power. When available, specially loaded 7.62×51mm Match ammunition enhances accuracy of the sniping rifle even more.

Among the 7.62×51mm rounds that have been loaded for US military use are: Ball, M59, the initial 7.62×51mm NATO loading which used a 150.5-grain (9.8g) bullet; High Pressure Test, M60, which was a proof load identified by its silver case; Armor Piercing M61, also 150.5 grains (9.8g), with a black tip; Tracer, M62, a 142-grain (9.2g) bullet, orange tip; Dummy, M63, used for training in loading the weapon and dry firing, with six longitudinal flutes on the cartridge case; Grenade M64, case mouth closed with a crimp and sealed with red lacquer; Ball, M80, a 147-grain (9.5g) bullet; Match, M118, a 173-grain (11.2g) full-metal-jacket boat-tail round designed for Match shooting; Ball, Special M118LR, a 175-grain (11.3g) hollow-point boat-tail round developed for long-range sniping; Frangible, M160, a 108.5-grain (7.0g) bullet designed to disintegrate upon hitting a hard target; Match M852, a 168-grain (10.9g) bullet designed for use in US National Matches but also used by snipers; Long Range, Mk 316 Mod 0, a 175-grain (11.3g) Sierra MatchKing hollow-point boat-tail round for long-range sniping; and Ball Barrier, T62TNB1 Mk 319 Mod 0, a 130-grain (8.4g) bullet designed for maximum performance and less muzzle flash in short-barreled carbines. A relatively recent development is the L2R2 round for the US Coast Guard to use when patrolling harbors. This cartridge was designed to defeat 6.35mm (.25in) mild steel at 200m (219yd) and to be lethal against soft targets to 400m (437yd), but to have a range of only 1,500m–2,000m (1,640–2,187yd). There have been numerous other experimental US 7.62×51mm loadings, as well as numerous service loadings in other countries using the cartridge.

Because the 7.62×51mm round has continued to be used in US sniping rifles, a bit more should be said about the M118, which was issued for use at the US National Rifle Matches but also for sniper usage. When the M118 Match ammunition was developed, the goal was to produce a round similar in performance to the M72 .30-06 round used in National Match M1 Garand rifles. Production and quality control were substantially stricter on M118 cartridges than on standard ball ammunition. Both the core (lead) and bullet jacket (90 percent copper and 10 percent zinc) were produced to strict tolerances. Bullets went through a three-station weighing machine, with bullets under 172.6 grains (11.18g) removed at station one. Bullets between 172.6 grains and 174.5 grains (11.3g) were removed at station two, and bullets over 174.5 grains were accumulated at station three (Poyer 2000: 42). Consistency of bullet weight is important so that each round will consistently impact at the same point.

Vietnam-era Marines in the jungle armed with M14 rifles. In the mid-1960s, the standard ammunition load in the USMC was five 20-round magazines for each rifleman and eight 20-round magazines for the automatic rifleman. (NARA)

Care was taken in manufacture of the M118 case and primer, with case dimensions held to a tight tolerance and the priming pellet within the primer weighed for consistency of weight, with a dry weight of .50 grains (.03g) the standard and variations of only .08 grains (.005g) allowed. Consistency of primer performance also affected the impact point of the bullet. Propellant consistency is the third component in consistency of bullet impact point. The standard deviation in velocity allowed in M118 rounds was 28ft/sec (8.3m/sec). Pressure was also checked for consistency (Poyer 2000: 43). A special loading press that produced 2,000 rounds per hour was used to ensure quality and consistency in the M118 rounds. As the Match rounds were produced, samples were tested for velocity, pressure, accuracy, and functioning in a National Match rifle (Poyer 2000: 44).

A military version of the very accurate civilian 168-grain (10.89g) Match load was developed for sniping and designated the M852. It was quite accurate, but not sufficiently so after 900yd (823m) due to the drop in velocity. To give the sniper using the 7.62×51mm round more range, the M118LR (long range) load was developed using a 175-grain (11.34g) boat-tail, hollow-point Match bullet. According to John Plaster, in a test by Lake City Army Ammunition Plant, using machine test barrels, this load fired a 12.09in (307mm) group at 1,000yd (914m), substantially better than either the M852 or M118 LR (Plaster 2008: 591).

In *Jane's Infantry Weapons, 2007–2008*, the cartridge identification tables give the standard dimensions for the 7.62×51mm NATO round as: case length 51.2mm (2.015in), bullet diameter 7.8mm (.308in), rim diameter 11.9mm (.470in), body diameter 11.9mm (.470in), and neck diameter 8.4mm (.350in) (Jones & Ness 2007: 602). Note that 7.62×51mm rounds manufactured to NATO specifications are marked as part of the head stamp with the symbol of a cross in a circle.

Once adopted, the round was chambered in some of the finest military rifles ever built. During the Cold War era, the two most widely used rifles in the West were the FN FAL and the HK G3 – by somewhere around 90–100 countries for the former and 65–70 for the latter. Many countries produced the rifles on license. Among other battle rifles chambered for the 7.62×51mm round were the Italian BM59, Israeli Galil, Swiss AMT, ArmaLite AR-10, Spanish CETME (basically the G3), FN-SCAR-H (Heavy), and HK417. The 7.62×51mm has also proven a very popular caliber for sniping rifles, among the best-known of which are: Accuracy International Arctic Warfare; Blaser 93 Tactical; FN Special Police Rifle; French FR F1 and F2; HK PSG1; Remington Modular Sniping Rifle; SAKO TRG; SIG SSG2000 and SSG3000; Steyr SSG; and Walther WA2000. To give an idea of the 7.62×51mm round's popularity, *Jane's* devotes four pages to listing contractors in various countries that load the cartridge.

Designed for competition shooters in the US National Matches, Springfield Armory's National Match M1A, shown here, incorporates features such as an air-gauged National Match medium-weight barrel, custom Match grade recoil-spring guide, National Match gas-system assembly, National Match front sight, National Match hooded rear-sight assembly, National Match trigger assembly and flash suppressor; the action and barrel are custom glass-bedded in a Match grade American walnut stock. The Loaded M1A has many of the same Match features of the National Match M1A but offers the option of a black composite stock instead of the walnut one used on the National Match M1A. The Super Match M1A improves on the National Match version with a rear lugged receiver, ultra-heavy air-gauged National Match barrel, custom oversized operating-rod guide, and Match grade walnut or McMillan fiberglass stock. (Springfield Armory)

THE M14 IN CIVILIAN HANDS

Today, the US civilian market for semiautomatic versions of the M14 remains strong and has done much to keep interest in the rifle alive. However, due to the fact that the M14 is a select-fire rifle, it can only be sold as a registered National Firearms Act (NFA) weapon. This has generated a large market for semiautomatic versions built on receivers specifically manufactured for semiautomatic rifles. According to Iannamico, as of 2005, there had been at least 350,000 semiautomatic M14-type rifles produced for US civilian sales by up to a dozen manufacturers (Iannamico 2005: 343). Although generically these rifles are often termed the "M1A," this is actually the designation for the Springfield Armory version, which has been the most popular and most widely distributed. While many civilian purchasers like the standard M1A, which resembles the original military-issue M14, many of the contractors that build DMRs or EBRs for the US armed forces will also build semiautomatic versions for civilian sales. Though expensive, these are quite popular.

US manufacturers

Of the semiautomatic versions produced in the USA, by far the largest number have come from Springfield Armory: 200,000 since 1971 (Iannamico 2005: 343). Among early purchasers

were those who wanted to shoot an M14-type rifle in High Power Rifle Matches. In 1974, the M1A was sanctioned for Matches by the NRA.

The original Springfield Armory rifles were produced by Elmer Balance of the L.H. Gun Company of Divine, Texas, under the Springfield Armory name, which could be used because the government Springfield Armory had closed in 1968 (Iannamico 2005: 343–45). Between 1971 and 1974, fewer than 3,000 M1A rifles were produced in Texas. These are highly sought by aficionados of the M1A. M1A receivers were made by Valley Ordnance using machinery purchased from Winchester. However, Valley Ordnance used investment-cast receivers rather than forged ones as produced for the M14. To meet the requirements of the Bureau of Alcohol, Tobacco, Firearms and Explosives (ATF), the new receivers were designed so that components to allow select-fire could not be installed. Using these receivers and some other parts produced by Valley Ordnance, Springfield Armory produced the finished M1A rifles. Most of the parts used in these early rifles were surplus M14 parts that were readily available, especially from H&R. Later, some parts were obtained from Israel when that country's M14s were declared surplus, though the complete rifles could not be imported into the United States (Iannamico 2005: 348–50).

In 1974, the new owners of Springfield Armory moved to Genesco, Illinois, where the company is still located today. In 1996, Springfield Armory also purchased Valley Ordnance and moved the machines to produce receivers at Genesco. During the production of the M1A at Genesco, Springfield Armory has offered a variety of models. Initially, the Standard M1A was based on the military-issue M14 rifle; at the time of writing, various stock options are offered that diverge from the original M14 look. These include: the National Match M1A; the Loaded M1A; the Super Match M1A; the SOCOM 16; the SOCOM II; the Scout Squad; and the M21 Tactical.

Springfield Armory's SOCOM 16, the short-barreled version of the M1A used by some law-enforcement agencies as a patrol rifle. Designed as a handier version of the Standard M1A, the SOCOM 16 has a 16in barrel, a proprietary muzzle brake, tritium front sight, and a forward rail for mounting optical sights; this rifle can serve for military and law-enforcement special-operations units. (Springfield Armory)

The author shooting Springfield Armory's SOCOM II; the optical sight is a Trijicon ACOG. The SOCOM II uses the shorter barrel of the SOCOM 16 but with full-length top rail and with side rails; its rear sight is an enlarged military aperture (Ghost Ring) adjustable, and it has a two-stage military trigger with a pull between 5lb and 6lb. Springfield Armory also offers the Scout Squad which, with a barrel length of 18in, falls between the 22in Standard M1A and the SOCOM rifles; as with the SOCOM 16, the Scout Squad incorporates a forward-mounted rail, while use of the forward-mounted optical sight offers a better field of view and allows the military or special law-enforcement operator to scan for targets more readily. (Author)

After Springfield Armory, the best-known producer of semiautomatic M14s is probably the Fulton Armory, which does upgrade work as well as producing its own rifle using receivers that are investment-cast and machined to Springfield Armory's specifications by a subcontractor. Some Fulton Armory semiautomatic M14s incorporate features that appeal to civilian shooters and collectors. For example, one version includes a non-functioning selector switch to give the rifle the appearance of a military-issue M14. Also available is a version legal for civilian purchasers that incorporates the features of the Mk 14 Mod 0 EBR (Iannamico 2005: 369–71).

Another company which produced a semiautomatic variant of the M14 was SEI. This company also manufactured receivers for use in building semiautomatic M14 copies. At one point SEI offered a carbine version of the M14 with 13in barrel known as the M14K. To overcome the muzzle flash, muzzle blast, and recoil, SEI developed a variation of the M60 GPMG gas system for the M14K and also a muzzle brake to control flash and recoil. This muzzle brake was long enough that when permanently attached it allowed the semiautomatic carbines to be sold as non-NFA weapons with a 16in barrel. Select-fire versions were also offered. Iannamico states that SEI made a total of 176 select-fire M14s, presumably including both rifles and carbines (Iannamico 2005: 363). As discussed earlier, SEI has performed conversions of many M14s for the US armed forces as well.

Another company which has produced semiautomatic versions of the M14 is Armscorp, which used SEI receivers at one point in the 1980s but now produces its own receivers made from 8620 steel investment castings heat-treated and tolerances held to current GI specifications. Originally, as did other manufacturers, Armscorp used surplus government-issue M14 parts.

Foreign-produced M14s

The Type 57 rifle produced by the Republic of China (Taiwan) has already been discussed, but another version of the M14 was also produced in the People's Republic of China (PRC). Most Favored Nation status during the 1980s allowed the PRC to export semiautomatic AK-47-type rifles and other small arms to the USA for sale on the civilian market. To take advantage of this lucrative market, the Chinese also started to produce semiautomatic versions of the M14 at Poly Technologies and The China North Industries Corporation (Norinco). These two companies were already well-known for the AK-47 rifles which had been imported into the USA, with Poly Tech rifles being considered of especially high quality. Chinese M14 copies were available at prices as low as half that of Springfield Armory or other US semiautomatic versions. Another consideration in regards to the PRC M14 copies is that parts are made to metric dimensions. As a result, most US-made parts will not fit without alteration.

The quality of the M14 clones produced by Poly Tech and Norinco was not always high, with problems in heat treatment and headspace most often cited. Fit of the rifles within their stocks was frequently poor as well. Both Poly Tech and Norinco receivers reportedly tested much softer on the Rockwell scale – a scale based on the indentation hardness of a material – than US receivers, with Norinco receivers being especially soft. However, Emerson states that with the cooperation of Poly Tech SEI tested some receivers and found them too hard, but that the Chinese corrected this problem. SEI noted other problems with the bolt lugs being too narrow and the hardness being unsatisfactory. These problems do not seem to have been addressed (Emerson 2007: 195). Since many US shooters had purchased the M14S, as the Poly Tech and Norinco copies were sometimes known, SEI and Fulton Armory offered upgrades on the PRC-made rifles to cater to them. Frequently these services included checking the rifles for headspace and general safety and replacing some Chinese parts such as the operating rod with US government-issue ones; however, note the comments above about US parts fitting Chinese rifles. To conform to various US import requirements, Poly Tech and Norinco weapons at various times were made without flash suppressors and bayonet lugs or with other features to make them less "military." Emerson argues that the Chinese-made barrels are of quite good quality. Because of their experience in producing chromium-plated barrels for AK-47 rifles, their M14 chromium-plated barrels are of high standard and capable of quite good accuracy (Emerson 2007: 218).

There have been rumors that the PRC M14 copy was not initially made for US export, but that the rifles were produced initially during the 1970s for use by guerrilla groups in the Philippines, along with 7.62×51mm ammunition with fake British head stamps (Johnson & Nelson 2010: 989). The idea seems to have been that guerrillas would be able to use captured 7.62×51mm ammunition in the rifles and that their source would be obscure. Some sources also claim that these Chinese copies were reverse-engineered from US M14 rifles captured during the Vietnam War. According to Lee Emerson, this reverse engineering occurred in 1965. Even US serial numbers were used. Various attempts were made to land the Chinese M14s in the Philippines, with only a small number ever being successfully supplied to the Philippine New People's Army guerrillas. Later, the remainder of the reported 100,000 rifles produced were disassembled, with some receivers converted to semiautomatic for export to Canada and New Zealand, while the remainder of the receivers were destroyed and the remaining parts sold to the USA (Emerson 2007: 189–90).

CONCLUSION

The history of the M14 rifle cannot be understood without accepting that it was a weapon whose origins were surrounded by political infighting. Even its most successful aspect, the 7.62×51mm NATO round, was only adopted after strenuous disagreements with NATO allies over the choice of a standard caliber. The USA's staunchest ally, Britain, battled for the acceptance of the .280 British round and the EM-2 "bullpup" rifle. As the most powerful member of NATO, the USA used its power to force the 7.62×51mm round on its allies. In retrospect, this has proven an excellent cartridge, one that continues in widespread use today. Still, its adoption was fraught with political leverage and negotiation. Political infighting continued among NATO allies over the adoption of a standard infantry rifle. Many US allies were left with the understanding that by the United States' acquiescence in the adoption of the 7.62×51mm cartridge, the USA would adopt the FN FAL rifle. Though the USA did test the FAL, it was the M14 that was adopted.

Within the US ordnance bureaucracy were factions that supported – to a greater or lesser extent – the goal of developing a modern .30-caliber lightweight battle rifle with detachable high-capacity magazine and select-fire capability. Included were powerful figures such as Colonel Rene Studler, Chief of Small Arms Research and Development for the US Army Ordnance Department (known after 1950 as the Ordnance Corps) from 1942 to 1953, John Garand, and others. Some believed that the M1 Garand could be altered to fire the 7.62×51mm round, use a detachable magazine, and fire on full-automatic. With the need for rifles during the Korean War, some Springfield Armory staff members found confirmation for their view that a new rifle based on the basic M1 Garand design was most desirable. Colonel Studler had thrown much of his influence behind the T25 rifle designed by Earle Harvey. Though this design showed promise, it was undermined by those at Springfield Armory with a bias toward an updated M1 Garand.

By 1952, the primary candidates for the new US service rifle appeared to be the T44 and the T48 (FN FAL). Having moved on from the T25, Earle Harvey had become the head of the Springfield Armory R&D (research and development) unit for handguns and rifles. Lloyd Corbett had played an important part in the development of the T44 and continued to work on the design as it evolved into the T44E4, which would be adopted as the M14 rifle. At least one argument in favor of adopting the M14 had been that much of the machinery used in producing the M1 Garand could still be used – this proved to be untrue. The adoption of the M14 played well politically as it was a US design, but it certainly did not please FN or NATO allies, none of whom would adopt the M14, while many adopted the FAL.

Even while the M14 was being developed and before it entered production, another constituency within the US armed forces was lobbying for a lighter rifle fabricated of modern materials and chambered for a 5.56-caliber round. Part of the early impetus for the 5.56×45mm round was the inability to control the 7.62×51mm round in the M14 when fired on full-automatic. The lower recoil of the 5.56×45mm round in the M16 rifle allowed far better control during full-automatic fire, thus helping realize the goal of an individual infantry firearm that allowed the infantrymen a fully automatic weapon.

July 2010: Cadets at the US Naval Academy at Annapolis, Maryland parade with shouldered M14s. (USN)

Just at the point when the AR-15/M16 was being considered for adoption, the United States was becoming engaged in a counterinsurgency campaign in Vietnam. Engagement ranges were generally shorter than those in Korea or Western Europe, and it was primarily an infantry war in a tropical climate. Additionally, the enemy was smaller of stature and US forces did not require a round with as much stopping power to put them down. As a result, the lightness of the M16 and the ability to carry substantially more spare magazines were important factors in its adoption.

Based on conversations with veterans from the period when the M14 was on issue and during the transition period to the M16 and to documentary accounts, a substantial portion of troops preferred the M14 and were willing to tolerate the additional weight. Nevertheless, within a little over a decade of its introduction, the M14 had been replaced.

An irony of the M14 story is its continued use as a sniping rifle and DMR, as one of the initial criticisms of the rifle was its lack of accuracy. However, the 20-round magazine capacity and self-loading action made the XM21/M21 a successful sniping rifle, though it was eventually replaced by precision bolt-action rifles. New wars in mountain and desert, however, caused the resurgence of the M14 due to its longer range and greater striking power.

As this is written, a substantial number of DMRs, EBRs, and other adaptations of the M14 continue to serve with US armed forces. For the most part, these are based on M14 rifles that went into storage decades ago only to be pulled from armories and given new life during the "War on Terror." For a rifle that has often been deemed a failure, the M14 has had a surprisingly long life. It has remained on issue in some form or other for a half-century and appears likely to be around for many more years. Grandsons and granddaughters of some of the soldiers armed with the M14 during the Cold War may now be armed with M14-based DMRs – maybe even the ones used by their grandfathers, but rebuilt.

BIBLIOGRAPHY

Anonymous (2013a). "T25," at Forgotten Weapons.com. http://www.
    forgottenweapons.com/m14-development/t25/ (accessed March
    4, 2014).

Anonymous (2013b). "The Designated Marksman Equation," at Pro
    Patria, Inc. http://pro-patria.us/designated_marksman (accessed
    March 4, 2014).

Bowden, Mark (1999). *Blackhawk Down*. London: Corgi.

Culbertson, John (2006). "Operation Tuscaloosa," in *War Story*,
    16 October 2006. (http://www.vietnamgear.com/Article.
    aspx?Art=102 (accessed March 4, 2014).

Duff, Scott A. & John M. Miller (2001). *The M14 Owner's Guide and
    Match Conditioning Instructions*. Export, PA: Scott A. Duff
    Publications.

Earhart, Major Thomas P. (2009). *Increasing Smalls Arms Lethality in
    Afghanistan: Taking Back the Infantry Half-Kilometer*. Fort
    Leavenworth, KS: School of Advanced Military Studies United
    States Army Command and General Staff College.

Eger, Christopher (2009). "Last of the Surviving M-14 Battle Rifles."
    http://suite101.com/a/last-of-the-surviving-m14-battle-
    rifles-a113682 (accessed March 4, 2014).

Emerson, Lee (2007). "M14 Rifle History and Development," Online
    Edition, June 3, 2007. http://photos.imageevent.com/badgerdog/
    generalstorage/m14tecnicalfolder/M14%20RHAD%20
    Online%20Edition%2020070603.pdf (accessed March 4, 2014).

Emerson, Lee (2010). "T44E4 versus FN FAL In the 1950s." http://
    ebrsopmods.proboards.com/thread/2699/t44e4-fn-fal-1950s
    (accessed March 4, 2014).

Ezell, Edward (1984). *The Great Rifle Controversy: Search for the
    Ultimate Infantry Weapon from World War II Through Vietnam
    and Beyond*. Harrisburg, PA: Stackpole Books.

Gourly, Scott (2003). "One Shot – Make It Count," in *Leatherneck*,
    January 28, 2003. http://www.leatherneck.com/forums/
    showthread.php?3857-One-Shot-Make-It-Count&s=479d3da7e4
    11d0c77969d589d829ae12 (accessed March 4, 2014).

Hallahan, William H. (1994). *Misfire: The History of How America's
    Small Arms Have Failed Our Military*. New York, NY: Charles
    Scribner's Sons.

Howe, Walter & E.H. Harrison (1963). "Making the M14 Rifle," in *The
    American Rifleman*, February 1963: pp. 13–20.

Howe, Walter J. & Colonel H. Harrison, US Army (Ret'd) (1961). "The
    M14 Rifle: A complete and detailed report on the status of the
    nation's new shoulder arm," in *The American Rifleman*, October
    1961: pp. 17–27.

Iannamico, Frank (2005). *The Last Steel Warrior: The U.S. M14 Rifle*.
    Henderson, NV: Moose Lake Publishing.

Johnston, Gary Paul & Thomas B. Nelson (2010). *The World's Assault Rifles*. Lorton, VA: Ironside International Publishers, Inc.

Jones, Charles A. (2005). "Phased out in the 1960s, M14 was 'very reliable,'" Leatherneck.com, The Lore of the Corps, December 12, 2005. http://www.leatherneck.com/forums/showthread. php?24034-Phased-out-in-1960s-M14-was-%91very-reliable%92 (accessed March 4, 2014).

Jones, Richard D. & Leland Ness, eds (2007). *Jane's Infantry Weapons, 2007–2008*. Coulsdon: Jane's Information Group.

Mangione, Sergeant First Class Jeremy (2010). "Bridging the Gap – the Designated Marksman," *Army Strong*, June 10, 2010. http:// armystrongstories.com/army-stories/bridging-the-gap-the-designated-marksman#.U06jUMfZA4B (accessed on April 23, 2014).

Pisor, Robert (1982). *The End of the Line: The Siege of Khe Sanh*. New York, NY: W.W. Norton & Co.

Plaster, Major John L. (2008). *The History of Sniping and Sharpshooting*. Boulder, CO: Paladin Press.

Poyer, Joe (2000). *The M-14 Type Rifle: A Shooter's and Collector's Guide*. Tustin, CA: North Cape Publications, Inc.

Smith Enterprises Incorporated (no date). "M14SE "CRAZY HORSE"® SQUAD DESIGNATED MARKSMAN (M14SE SDM) AND MK14 SEI RIFLE." http://www.smithenterprise.com/products02. html (accessed March 4, 2014).

Stevens, R. Blake (1995). *U.S. Rifle M14 from John Garand to the M21*. Cobourg: Collector Grade Publications.

Tompkins, John S. (1963). "The U.S. Army's Blunderbuss Bungle That Fattened Your Taxes," in *True Magazine*, April 1963.

US Army (1962a). *Rifle Evaluation Study*. Infantry Combat Development Agency.

US Army (1962b). *Rifle Evaluation Study (U)*. United States Army Combat Developments Command.

US Army (1965). *Department of the Army Field Manual FM 23-8. U.S. Rifle 7.62mm, M14 and M14E2*. Washington, DC: Headquarters, Department of the Army.

US Army (1967). *Small Arms Use in Vietnam: M14 Rifle and .45-Caliber Pistol*, U.S. Army Technical Note 1-67. Aberdeen Proving Ground, MD: Human Engineering Laboratories.

US Army (1974). *Field Manual M14 and M14A1 Rifles and Rifle Marksmanship, FM 23-8*. Washington, DC: Headquarters, Department of the Army.

US Army Marksmanship Unit (no date). http://www.usaac.army.mil/ amu/training/sdm.asp (accessed April 23, 2014).

INDEX

Figures in **bold** refer to illustrations.